TWELVE SERMONS

PLAN OF SALVATION

DELIVERED
AT THE METROPOLITAN TABERNACLE

BY

C. H. SPURGEON

BAKER BOOK HOUSE
Grand Rapids, Michigan

Paperback edition issued 1976
by Baker Book House Company

ISBN: 0-8010-8085-1

First printing, December 1976
Second printing, November 1977

PHOTOLITHOPRINTED BY CUSHING - MALLOY, INC.
ANN ARBOR, MICHIGAN, UNITED STATES OF AMERICA
1977

Contents

Salvation to the Uttermost

" Wherefore he is able also to save them to the uttermost that come unto God by him, seeing he ever liveth to make intercession for them."—Hebrews vii. 25.

SALVATION is a doctrine peculiar to revelation. Revelation affords us a complete history of it, but nowhere else can we find any trace thereof. God has written many books, but only one book has had for its aim the teaching of the ways of mercy. He has written the great book of creation, which it is our duty and our pleasure to read. It is a volume embellished on its surface with starry gems and rainbow colours, and containing in its inner leaves marvels at which the wise may wonder for ages, and yet find a fresh theme for their conjectures. Nature is the spelling-book of man, in which he may learn his Maker's name, he hath studded it with embroidery, with gold, with gems. There are doctrines of truth in the mighty stars, and there are lessons written on the green earth and in the flowers upspringing from the sod. We read the books of God when we see the storm and tempest, for all things speak as God would have them; and if our ears are open we may hear the voice of God in the rippling of every rill, in the roll of every thunder, in the brightness of every lightning, in the twinkling of every star, in the budding of every flower. God has written the great book of creation, to teach us what he is—how great, how mighty. But I read nothing of salvation in creation. The rocks tell me, "Salvation is not in us;" the winds howl, but they howl not salvation: the waves rush upon the shore, but among the wrecks which they wash up, they reveal no trace of salvation; the fathomless caves of ocean bear pearls, but they bear no pearls of grace; the starry heavens have their flashing meteors, but they have no voices of salvation. I find salvation written nowhere, till in this volume of my Father's grace I find his blessed love unfolded towards the great human family, teaching them that they are lost, but that he can save them, and that in saving them he can be "just, and yet the justifier of the ungodly." Salvation, then, is to be found in the Scriptures, and in the Scriptures only; for we can read nothing of it elsewhere. And while it is to be found only in Scripture, I hold that the peculiar doctrine of revelation is salvation. I believe that the Bible was sent not to teach me history, but to teach me grace—not to give me a system of philosophy, but to give me a system of divinity—not to teach worldly wisdom, but spiritual wisdom. Hence I hold all preaching of philosophy and science in the pulpit to be altogether out of place. I would check no man's liberty in this matter, for God only is the Judge of man's conscience; but it is my firm opinion that if we profess to be Christians, we are bound to keep to Christianity; if we profess to be Christian ministers, we drivel away the Sabbath-day, we mock our hearers, we insult God, if we deliver lectures upon botany, or geology, instead of delivering sermons on salvation. He who does not always preach the gospel, ought not to be accounted a true-called minister of God.

Well, then it is salvation I desire to preach to you. We have, in our text, two or three things. In the first place, we are told *who they are who will be saved,* " them that come unto God by Jesus Christ;" in the second place we are told *the extent of the Saviour's ability to save,* " he is able to save to the uttermost;" and in the third place, we have *the reason given why he can save,* " seeing he ever liveth to make intercession for them."

1. First, we are told THE PEOPLE WHO ARE TO BE SAVED. And the people who are to be saved are "those who come unto God by Jesus Christ." There is no limitation here of sect or denomination: it does not say, the Baptist, the Independent, or the Episcopalian that comes unto God by Jesus Christ, but it simply says, "*them,*" by which I understand men of all creeds, men of all ranks, men of all classes, who do but come to Jesus Christ. They shall be saved, whatever their apparent position before men, or whatever may be the denomination to which they have linked themselves.

1. Now, I must have you notice, in the first place, *where these people come to.* They "come unto God." By coming to God we are not to understand the mere formality of devotion, since this may be but a solemn means of sinning. What a splendid general confession is that in the Church of England Prayer Book: " We have erred and strayed from thy ways like lost sheep ; we have done those things which we ought not to have done, and we have left undone those things which we ought to have done, and there is no health in us." There is not to be found a finer confession in the English language. And yet how often, my dear friends, have the best of us mocked God by repeating such expressions verbally, and thinking we have done our duty ! How many of you go to chapel, and must confess your own absence of mind while you have bowed your knee in prayer, or uttered a song of praise ! My friends, it is one thing to go to church or chapel; it is quite another thing to go *to God.* There are many people who can pray right eloquently, and who do so ; who have learned a form of prayer by heart, or, perhaps, use an extemporary form of words of their own composing: but who, instead of going to God, are all the while going from God. Let me persuade you all not to be content with mere formality. There will be many damned who never broke the Sabbath, as they thought, but who, all their lives were Sabbath-breakers. It is as much possible to break the Sabbath in a church as it is to break the Sabbath in the park ; it is as easy to break it here in this solemn assembly as in your own houses. Every one of you virtually break the Sabbath when you merely go through a round of duties, having done which, you retire to your chambers, fully content with yourselves, and fancy that all is over—that you have done your day's work—whereas, you have never come to God at all, but have merely come to the outward ordinance and to the visible means, which is quite another thing from coming to God himself.

And let me tell you, again, that coming *to God* is not what some of you suppose— *now and then sincerely performing an act of devotion, but giving to the world the greater part of your life.* You think that if sometimes you are sincere, if now and then you put up an earnest cry to heaven, God will accept you; and though your life may be still worldly, and your desires still carnal, you suppose that for the sake of this occasional devotion God will be pleased, in his infinite mercy, to blot out your sins. I tell you, sinners, there is no such thing as bringing half of yourselves to God, and leaving the other half away. If a man has come here, I suppose he has brought his whole self with him; and so, if a man comes to God, he cannot come, half of him, and half of him stay away. Our whole being must be surrendered to the service of our Maker. We must come to him with an entire dedication of ourselves, giving up all we are, and all we ever shall be, to be thoroughly devoted to his service, otherwise we have never come to God aright. I am astonished to see how people in these days try to love the world and love Christ too; according to the old proverb, they "hold with the hare and run with the hounds." They are real good Christians sometimes, when they think they ought to be religious; but they are right bad fellows at other seasons, when they think that religion would be a litttte loss to them. Let me warn you all. It is of no earthly use for you to pretend to be on two sides of the question. "If God be God, serve him; If Baal be God, serve him." I like an out-and-out man of any sort. Give me a man that is a sinner: I have some hope for him when I see him sincere in his vices, and open in acknowledging his own character ; but if you give me a man who is half-hearted, who is not quite bold enough to be all for the devil, nor quite sincere enough to be all for Christ, I tell you, I despair of such a man as that. The man who wants to link the two together is in an extremely hopeless case. Do you think, sinners, you will be able to serve two masters, when Christ has said you cannot? Do you fancy you can walk with God and walk with mammon too? Will you take God on one arm, and the devil on the other? Do you suppose you can be allowed to drink the cup of the Lord, and the cup of Satan at the same time? I tell you, ye shall depart, as cursed and miserable hypocrites, if so you come to God. God will have the whole of you come, or else you shall not come at all. The whole man must seek after the Lord; the whole soul must be poured out before him; otherwise it is no acceptable coming to God at all. Oh, halters between two opinions, remember this and tremble.

I think I hear one say, "Well, then, tell us what it is to come to God." I answer, coming to God implies, *leaving something else.* If a man comes to God, he must leave his sins; he must leave his righteousness; he must leave both his bad works and his good ones, and come to God, leaving them entirely.

Again, coming to God implies, *that there is no aversion towards him ;* for a man will not come to God while he hates God; he will be sure to keep away. Coming to God signifies having *some love to God.* Again: coming to God signifies *desiring God,* desiring to be near to him. And, above all, it signifies *praying to God and putting faith in him.* That is coming to God; and those that have come to God in that fashion are among the saved. They come *to God :* that is the place to which their eager spirits hasten.

2. But notice, next, *how they come.* They "come unto God *by Jesus Christ.*" We have known many persons who call themselves natural religionists. They worship the God of nature, and they think that they can approach God apart from Jesus Christ. There be some men we wot of who despise the mediation of the Saviour, and, who, if they were in an hour of peril, would put up their prayer at once to God, without faith in the Mediator. Do such of you fancy that you will be heard and saved by the great God your Creator, apart from the merits of his Son? Let me solemnly assure you, in God's most holy name, there never was a prayer answered for salvation, by God the Creator, since Adam fell, without Jesus Christ the Mediator. "No man can come unto God but by Jesus Christ;" and if any one of you deny the Divinity of Christ, and if any soul among you do not come to God through the merits of a Saviour, bold fidelity obliges me to pronounce you condemned persons; for however amiable you may be, you cannot be right in the rest, unless you think rightly of him. I tell you, ye may offer all the prayers that ever may be prayed, but ye shall be damned, unless ye put them up through Christ. It is all in vain for you to take your prayers and carry them yourself to the throne. "Get thee hence, sinner; get thee hence," says God; "I never knew thee. Why didst not thou put thy prayer into the hands of a Mediator? It would have been sure of an answer. But as thou presentest it thyself, see what I will do with it!" And he reads your petition, and casts it to the four winds of heaven; and thou goest away unheard, unsaved. The Father will never save a man apart from Christ; there is not one soul now in heaven who was not saved by Jesus Christ; there is not one who ever came to God aright, who did not come through Jesus Christ. If you would be at peace with God, you must come to him through Christ, as the way, the truth, and the life, making mention of his righteousness, and of his only.

3. But when these people come, *what do they come for ?* There are some who think they come to God, who do not come for the right thing. Many a young student cries to God to help him in his studies; many a merchant comes to God that he may be guided through a dilemma in his business. They are accustomed, in any difficulty, to put up some kind of prayer, which, if they knew its value, they might cease from offering, for "the sacrifice of the wicked is an abomination to the Lord." But the poor sinner, in coming to Christ, has only one object. If all the world were offered to him, he would not think it worth his acceptance if he could not have Jesus Christ. There is a poor man, condemned to die, locked up in the condemned cell: the bell is tolling: he will soon be taken off to die on the gallows. There, man, I have brought you a fine robe. What! not smile at it? Look! it is stiff with silver! Mark you not how it is bedizened with jewels? Such a robe as that

cost many and many a pound, and much fine workmanship was expended on it. Contemptuously he smiles at it! See here, man, I present thee something else: here is a glorious estate for thee, with broad acres, fine mansions, parks and lawns; take that title deed, 'tis thine. What! not smile, sir? Had I given that estate to any man who walked the street, less poor than thou art, he would have danced for very joy. And wilt not thou afford a smile, when I make thee rich and clothe thee with gold? Then let me try once more. There is Cæsar's purple for thee; put it on thy shoulders—there is his crown; it shall sit on no other head but thine. It is the crown of empires that know no limit. I'll make thee a king; thou shalt have a kingdom upon which the sun shall never set; thou shalt reign from pole to pole. Stand up; call thyself Cæsar. Thou art emperor. What! no smile? What dost thou want? "Take away that bauble," says he of the crown; "rend up that worthless parchment; take away that robe; ay, cast it to the winds. Give it to the kings of the earth who live; but I have to die, and of what use are these to me? Give me a pardon, and I will not care to be a Cæsar. Let me live a beggar, rather than die a prince." So is it with the sinner when he comes to God: he comes for salvation. He says—

> "Wealth and honor I disdain;
> Earthly comforts, Lord, are vain,
> These will never satisfy,
> Give me Christ, or else I die."

Mercy is his sole request. O my friends, if you have ever come to God, crying out for salvation, and for salvation only, then you have come unto God aright. It were useless then to mock you. You cry for bread: should I give you stones? You would but hurl them at me. Should I offer you wealth? It would be little. We must preach to the sinner who comes to Christ, the gift for which he asks—the gift of salvation by Jesus Christ the Lord—as being his own by faith.

4. One more thought upon this coming to Christ. *In what style do these persons come?* I will try and give you a description of certain persons, all coming to the gate of mercy, as they think, for salvation. There comes one, a fine fellow in a coach and six! See how hard he drives, and how rapidly he travels; he is a fine fellow: he has men in livery, and his horses are richly caparisoned; he is rich, exceeding rich. He drives up to the gate, and says, "Knock at that gate for me; I am rich enough, but still I dare say it would be as well to be on the safe side; I am a very respectable gentleman; I have enough of my own good works and my own merits, and this chariot, I dare say, would carry me across the river death, and land me safe on the other side; but still, it is fashionable to be religious, so I will approach the gate. Porter! undo the gates, and let me in; see what an honorable man I am." You will never find the gates undone for that man; he does not approach in the right manner. There comes another; he has not quite so much merit, but still he has some; he comes walking along, and having leisurely marched up, he cries, "Angel! open the gate to me; I am come to Christ: I think I should like to be saved. I do not feel that I very much require salvation; I have always been a very honest, upright, moral man; I do not know myself to have been much of a sinner; I have robes of my own; but I would not mind putting Christ's robes on; it would not hurt me. I may as well have the wedding garment; then I can have mine own too." Ah! the gates are still hard and fast, and there is no opening of them. But let me show you the right man. There he comes, sighing and groaning, crying and weeping all the way. He has a rope on his neck, for he thinks he deserves to be condemned. He has rags on him, he comes to the heavenly throne; and when he approaches mercy's gate he is almost afraid to knock. He lifts up his eyes and he sees it written, "Knock, and it shall be opened to you;" but he fears lest he should profane the gate by his poor touch; he gives at first a gentle rap, and if mercy's gate open not, he is a poor dying creature; so he gives another rap, then another and another; and although he raps times without number, and no answer comes, still he is a sinful man, and he knows himself to be unworthy; so he keeps rapping still; and at last the good angel smiling from the gate, says, "Ah! this gate was built for beggars not for princes; heaven's gate was made for spiritual paupers, not for rich men

Christ died for sinners, not for those who are good and excellent. He came into the world to save the vile.

Not the righteous,—
Sinners, Jesus came to call.'

Come in, poor man! Come in. Thrice welcome!" And the angels sing, " Thrice welcome!" How many of you, dear friends, have come to God by Jesus Christ in that fashion? Not with the pompous pride of the Pharisee, not with the cant of the good man who thinks he deserves salvation, but with the sincere cry of a penitent, with the earnest desire of a thirsty soul after living water, panting as the thirsty hart in the wilderness after the water-brooks, desiring Christ as they that look for the morning; I say, more than they that look for the morning. As my God who sits in heaven liveth, if you have not come to God in this fashion, you have not come to God at all; but if you have thus come to God, here is the glorious word for you—" He is able to save to the uttermost them that come unto God by him."

II. Thus we have disposed of the first point, the coming to God; and now, secondly, WHAT IS THE MEASURE OF THE SAVIOUR'S ABILITY? This is a question as important as if it were for life or death—a question as to the ability of Jesus Christ. How far can salvation go? What are its limits and its boundaries? Christ is a Saviour: how far is he able to save? He is a Physician: to what extent will his skill reach to heal diseases? What a noble answer the text gives! "He is able to save to the uttermost." Now, I will certainly affirm, and no one can deny it, that no one here knows how far the uttermost is. David said, if he took the wings of the morning, to fly to the uttermost parts of the sea, even there should God reach him. But who knoweth where the uttermost is? Borrow the angel's wing, and fly far, far beyond the most remote star: go where wing has never flapped before, and where the undisturbed ether is as serene and quiet as the breast of Deity itself: you will not come to the uttermost. Go on still; mounted on a morning ray, fly on still, beyond the bounds of creation, where space itself fails, and where chaos takes up its reign: you will not come to the uttermost. It is too far for mortal intellect to conceive of; it is beyond the range of reason or of thought. Now, our text tells us that Christ is " able to save to the uttermost."

1. Sinner, I shall address thee first; and saints of God, I shall address you afterwards. Sinner, Christ is "able to save to the uttermost;" by which we understand that *the uttermost extent of guilt* is not beyond the power of the Saviour. Can any one tell what is the uttermost amount to which a man might sin? Some of us conceive that Palmer has gone almost to the uttermost of human depravity; we fancy that no heart could be much more vile than that which conceived a murder so deliberate, and contemplated a crime so protracted; but I can conceive it possible that there might be even worse men than he, and that if his life were spared, and he were set at large, he might become even a worse man than he is now. Yea, supposing he were to commit another murder, and then another, and another, would he have gone to the uttermost? Could not a man be yet more guilty? As long as ever he lives, he may become more guilty than he was the day before. But yet my text says, Christ is "able to save to the uttermost." I may imagine a person has crept in here, who thinks himself to be the most loathsome of all beings, the most condemned of all creatures. "Surely," says he, "I have gone to the utmost extremity of sin; none could outstrip me in vice." My dear friend, suppose you had gone to the uttermost, remember that even then you would not have gone beyond the reach of divine mercy; for he is "able to save to the uttermost," and it is possible that you yourself might go a little further, and therefore you have not gone to the uttermost yet. However far you may have gone—if you have gone to the very arctic regions of vice, where the sun of mercy seems to scatter but a few oblique rays, there can the light of salvation reach you. If I should see a sinner staggering on in his progress to hell, I would not give him up, even when he had advanced to the last stage of iniquity. Though his foot hung trembling over the very verge of perdition, I would not cease to pray for him; and though he should in his poor drunken wickedness go staggering on till one foot were over hell, and he were ready to perish, I would not despair of him. Till the pit had shut her mouth upon him I would believe it still possible that divine grace might save him. See there! he is just upon the edge of the

pit, ready to fall; but ere he falls, free grace bids, "Arrest that man!" Down mercy comes, catches him on her broad wings, and he is saved, a trophy of redeeming love. If there be any such in this vast assembly—if there be any here of the outcast of society, the vilest of the vile, the scum, the draff of this poor world,—oh! ye chief of sinners! Christ is "able to save to the uttermost." Tell that everywhere, in every garret, in every cellar, in every haunt of vice, in every kennel of sin; tell it everywhere! "To the uttermost!" "He is able also to save them to the uttermost."

3. Yet again: not only to the uttermost of crime, but *to the uttermost of rejection.* I must explain what I mean by this. There are many of you here who have heard the gospel from your youth up. I see some here, who like myself are children of pious parents. There are some of you upon whose infant forehead the pure heavenly drops of a mother's tears continually fell; there are many of you here who were trained up by one whose knee, whenever it was bent, was ever bent for you. She never rested in her bed at night till she had prayed for you, her first-born son. Your mother has gone to heaven. it may be, and all the prayers she ever prayed for you are as yet unanswered. Sometimes you wept. You remember well how she grasped your hand, and said to you, "Ah! John, you will break my heart by this your sin, if you continue running on in those ways of iniquity: oh! if you did but know how your mother's heart yearns for your salvation, surely your soul would melt, and you would fly to Christ." Do you not remember that time? The hot sweat stood upon your brow, and you said—for you could not break her heart— "Mother, I will think of it;" and you did think of it; but you met your companion outside, and it was all gone: your mother's expostulation was brushed away; like the thin cobwebs of the gossamer, blown by the swift north wind, not a trace of it was left. Since then you have often stepped in to hear the minister. Not long ago you heard a powerful sermon; the minister spoke as though he were a man just started from his grave, with as much earnestness as if he had been a sheeted ghost come back from the realms of despair, to tell you his own awful fate, and warn you of it. You remember how the tears rolled down your cheeks, while he told you of sin, of righteousness, and of judgment to come; you remember how he preached to **you** Jesus and salvation by the cross, and you rose up from your seat in that chapel, and you said, "Please God I am spared another day, I will turn to him with full purpose of heart." And there you are, still unchanged—perhaps worse than you were; and you have spent your Sunday afternoon the angel knows where: and your mother's spirit knows where you have spent it too, and could she weep, she would weep over you who have this day despised God's Sabbath, and trampled on his Holy Word. But dost thou feel in thine heart to-night the tender motions of the Holy Spirit? Dost thou feel something say, "Sinner! come to Christ now?" Dost thou hear conscience whispering to thee, telling thee of thy past transgression? And is there some sweet angel voice, saying, "Come to Jesus, come to Jesus; he will save you yet?" I tell you, sinner, you may have rejected Christ to the very uttermost; but he is still able to save you. There are **a** thousand prayers on which you have trampled, there are a hundred sermons all wasted on you, there are thousands of Sabbaths which you have thrown away; you have rejected Christ, you have despised his Spirit; but still he ceases not to cry, "Return, return!" He 's "able to save thee to the uttermost," if thou comest unto God by him.

3. There is another case which demands my particular attention to-night. It is that of the man who has gone *to the uttermost of despair.* There are some poor creatures in this world, who from a course of crime have become hardened, and when at last aroused by remorse and the prickings of conscience, there is an evil spirit which broods over them, telling them it is hopeless for such as they are to seek salvation. We have met with some who have gone so far that they have thought that even devils might be saved rather than they could. They have given themselves up for lost, and signed their own death-warrant, and in such a state of mind have positively taken the halter in their hand, to end their unhappy lives. Despair has brought many a man to a premature death; it hath sharpened many a knife, and mingled many a cup of poison. Have I a despairing person here? I know him by his sombre face and downcast looks. He wishes he were dead, for he thinks that hell itself could be scarce worse torment than to be here expecting it. Let me whisper to him words of consolation. Despairing soul! hope yet, for Christ ✦ is able to save to the uttermost;" and though thou art put in the lowest dungeon

of the castle of despair, though key after key hath been turned upon thee, and the iron grating of thy window forbids all filing, and the height of thy prison-wall is so awful that thou couldst not expect to escape, yet let me tell thee, there is one at the gate who can break every bolt, and undo every lock; there is one who can lead thee out to God's free air and save thee yet, for though the worst may come to the worst, he "is able to save thee to the uttermost."

4. And now a word to the saint, to comfort him: for this text is his also. Beloved brother in the gospel! Christ is able to save thee to the uttermost. Art thou brought very low by *distress*? hast thou lost house and home, friend and property? Remember, thou hast not come "to the uttermost" yet. Badly off as thou art, thou mightest be worse. He is able to save thee; and suppose it should come to this, that thou hadst not a rag left, nor a crust, nor a drop of water, still he would be able to save thee, for "he is able to save to the uttermost." So with temptation. If thou shouldst have the sharpest *temptation* with which mortal was ever tried, he is able to save thee. If thou shouldst be brought into such a predicament that the foot of the devil should be upon thy neck, and the fiend should say, "Now I will make an end of thee," God would be able to save thee then. Ay, and in the uttermost *infirmity* shouldst thou live for many a year, till thou art leaning on thy staff, and tottering along thy weary life, if thou shouldst outlive Methusaleh, thou couldst not live beyond the uttermost, and he would save thee then. Yea, and when thy little bark is launched by *death* upon the unknown sea of eternity, he will be with thee; and though thick vapours of gloomy darkness gather round thee, and thou canst not see into the dim future, though thy thoughts tell thee that thou wilt be destroyed, yet God will be "able to save thee to the uttermost."

Then, my friends, if Christ is able to save a Christian to the uttermost, do you suppose he will ever let a Christian perish? Wherever I go, I hope always to bear my hearty protest against the most accursed doctrine of a saint's falling away and perishing. There are some ministers who preach that a man may be a child of God (now, angels! do not hear what I am about to say, listen to me, ye who are down below in hell, for it may suit you) that a man may be a child of God to-day, and a child of the devil to-morrow; that God may acquit a man, and yet condemn him—save him by grace, and then let him perish—suffer a man to be taken out of Christ's hands, though he has said such a thing shall never take place. How will you explain this? It certainly is no lack of power. You must accuse him of a want of love, and will you dare to do that? He is full of love; and since he has also the power, he will never suffer one of his people to perish. It is true, and ever shall be true, that he will save them to the very uttermost.

III. Now, in the last place, WHY IS IT THAT JESUS CHRIST IS "ABLE TO SAVE TO THE UTTERMOST?" The answer is, that he "ever liveth to make intercession for them." This implies that *he died*, which is indeed the great source of his saving power. Oh! how sweet it is to reflect upon the great and wonderous works which Christ hath done, whereby he hath become "the high priest of our profession," able to save us! It is pleasant to look back to Calvary's hill, and to behold that bleeding form expiring on the tree; it is sweet, amazingly sweet, to pry with eyes of love between those thick olives, and hear the groanings of the Man who sweat great drops of blood. Sinner, if thou askest me how Christ can save thee, I tell thee this—he can save thee, because he did not save himself; he can save thee, because he took thy guilt and endured thy punishment. There is no way of salvation apart from the satisfaction of divine justice. Either the sinner must die, or else some one must die for him. Sinner, Christ can save thee, because, if thou comest to God by him, then he died for thee. God has a debt against us, and he never remits that debt; he will have it paid. Christ pays it, and then the poor sinner goes free.

And we are told another reason why he is able to save: not only because he died, but *because he lives to make intercession for us*. That Man who once died on the cross, is alive; that Jesus who was buried in the tomb is alive. If you ask me what he is doing, I bid you listen. Listen, if you have ears! Did you not hear him, poor penitent sinner? Did you not hear his voice, sweeter than harpers playing on their harps? Did you not hear a charming voice? Listen! what did it say? "O my Father! forgive —— !" Why, he mentioned your own name! "O my Father, forgive him; he knew not what he did. It is true he sinned against light, and knowledge, and warnings; sinned wilfully and woefully; but, Father, forgive him!" Penitent, if thou canst listen, thou wilt hear him praying for thee. And that is why he is able to save.

A warning and a question, and I have done. First, a warning. Remember, *there is a limit to God's mercy.* I have told you from the Scriptures, that "he is *able* to save to the uttermost;" but there is a limit to his purpose to save. If I read the Bible rightly, there is one sin which can never be forgiven. It is the sin against the Holy Ghost. Tremble, unpardoned sinners, lest ye should commit that. If I may tell you what I think the sin against the Holy Ghost is, I must say that I believe it to be different in different people; but in many persons, the sin against the Holy Ghost consists in stifling their convictions. Tremble, my hearers, lest to-night's sermon should be the last you hear. Go away and scorn the preacher, if you like; but do not neglect his warning. Perhaps the very next time thou laughest over a sermon, or mockest at a prayer, or despisest a text, the very next oath thou swearest, God may say, "He is given to idols, let him alone; my Spirit shall no more strive with that man; I will never speak to him again." That is the warning.

And now, lastly, the question. *Christ has done so much for you: what have you ever done for him?* Ah! poor sinner, if thou knewest that Christ died for thee—and I know that he did, if thou repentest—if thou knewest that one day thou wilt be his, wouldst thou spit upon him now? wouldst thou scoff at God's day, if thou knewest that one day it will be thy day? wouldst thou despise Christ, if thou knewest that he loves thee now, and will display that love by-and-by ? Oh! there are some of you that will loathe yourselves when you know Christ because you did not treat him better. He will come to you one of these bright mornings, and he will say, "Poor sinner, I forgive you;" and you will look up in his face, and say, "What! Lord, forgive me? I used to curse thee, I laughed at thy people, I despised every-thing that had to do with religion. Forgive me?" "Yes," says Christ, "give me thy hand; I loved thee when thou hatedst me: come here!" And sure there is nothing will break a heart half so much as thinking of the way in which you sinned against one who loved you so much.

Oh! beloved, hear again the text,—"He is able also to save to the uttermost them that come unto God by him." I am no orator, I have no eloquence; but if I were the one, and had the other, I would preach to you with all my soul. As it is, I only talk right on, and tell you what I do know; I can only say again,

> "He is able;
> He is willing: doubt no **more.**
>
> Come, ye thirsty, come and welcome,
>   God's free bounty glorify:
> True belief and true repentance,
>   Every grace that brings us nigh—
> Without money,
> Come to Jesus Christ, and buy."

For he is able also to save to the uttermost them that come unto God by him." O Lord! make sinners come! Spirit of God! make them come! Compel them to come to Christ by sweet constraint, and let not our words be in vain, or our labour lost; for Jesus Christ's sake! Amen.

Salvation of the Lord

"Salvation is of the Lord."—Jonah ii. 9.

JONAH learned this sentence of good theology in a strange college. He learned it in the whale's belly, at the bottom of the mountains, with the weeds wrapped about his head, when he supposed that the earth with her bars was about him for ever. Most of the grand truths of God have to be learned by trouble; they must be burned into us with the hot iron of affliction, otherwise we shall not truly receive them. No man is competent to judge in matters of the kingdom, until first he has been tried; since there are many things to be learned in the depths which we can never know in the heights. We discover many secrets in the caverns of the ocean, which, though we had soared to heaven, we never could have known. He shall best meet the wants of God's people as a preacher who has had those wants himself; he shall best comfort God's Israel who has needed comfort; and he shall best preach salvation who has felt his own need of it. Jonah, when he was delivered from his great danger, when by the command of God the fish had obediently left its great deeps and delivered its cargo upon dry land, was then capable of judging; and this was the result of his experience under his trouble—" Salvation is of the Lord."

By salvation here we do not merely understand the special salvation which Jonah received from death; for according to Dr. Gill, there is something so special in the original, in the word salvation having one more letter than it usually has, when it only refers to some temporary deliverance, that we can only understand it here as relating to the great work of the salvation of the soul which endureth for ever. That "Salvation is of the Lord," I shall this morning try to show as best I can. First, I shall endeavour to *explain the doctrine;* then I shall try to show you *how God has guarded us from making any mistakes, and has hedged us up to make us believe the gospel;* then I shall dwell upon *the influence of this truth upon men;* and shall close up by showing you *the counterpart of the doctrine.* Seeing every truth hath its obverse, so hath this.

I. First, then, to begin by explanation, let us EXPOUND THIS DOCTRINE—the doctrine that salvation is of the Lord, or of Jehovah. We are to understand by this, that the whole of the work whereby men are saved from their natural estate of sin and ruin, and are translated into the kingdom of God and made heirs of eternal happiness, is of God, and of him only. "Salvation is of the Lord."

To begin, then, at the beginning, *the plan of salvation is entirely of God.* No human intellect and no created intelligence assisted God in the planning of salvation; he contrived the way, even as he himself carried it out. The plan of sal-

13

ration was devised before the existence of angels. Before the day-star flung its ray across the darkness, when as yet the unnavigated ether had not been fanned by the wing of seraph, and when the solemnity of silence had never been disturbed by the song of angel, God had devised a way whereby he might save man, whom he foresaw would fall. He did not create angels to consult with them; no, of himself he did it. We might truly ask the question, "With whom took he counsel? Who instructed him, when he planned the great architecture of the temple of mercy? With whom took he counsel, when he digged the deeps of love, that out of them there might well up springs of salvation? Who aided him?" None. He himself, alone did it. In fact, if angels had then been in existence, they could not have assisted God; for I can well suppose that if a solemn conclave of those spirits had been held, if God had put to them this question, "Man will rebel; I declare I will punish; my justice, inflexible and severe, demands that I should do so; but yet I intend to have mercy;" if he had put the question to the celestial squadrons of mighty ones, "How can these things be? How can justice have its demands fulfilled, and how can mercy reign?" the angels would have sat in silence until now; they could not have dictated the plan; it would have surpassed angelic intellect to have conceived the way whereby righteousness and peace should meet together, and judgment and mercy should kiss each other. God devised it, because without God it could not have been devised. It is a plan too splendid to have been the product of any mind except of that mind which afterwards carried it out. "Salvation" is older than creation; it is "of the Lord."

And as it was of the Lord in planning, so *it was of the Lord in execution.* No one has helped to provide salvation; God has done it all himself. The banquet of mercy is served up by one host; that host is he to whom the cattle on a thousand hills belong. But none have contributed any dainties to that royal banquet; he hath done it all himself. The royal bath of mercy, wherein black souls are washed was filled from the veins of Jesus; not a drop was contributed by any other being. He died upon the cross, and as an expiator he died alone. No blood of martyrs mingleth with that stream; no blood of noble confessors and of heroes of the cross entered into the river of atonement; that is filled from the veins of Christ, and from nowhere else beside. He hath done it wholly. Atonement is the unaided work of Jesus. On yonder cross I see the man who "trod the winepress alone;" in yonder garden I see the solitary conqueror, who came to the fight single-handed, whose own arm brought salvation, and whose omnipotence sustained him. "Salvation is of the Lord," as to its provisions; Jehovah—Father, Son, and Spirit—hath provided everything.

So far we are all agreed; but now we shall have to separate a bit. "Salvation is of the Lord," *in the application of it.* "No," says the Arminian, "it is not; salvation is of the Lord, inasmuch as he does all for man that he can do; but there is something that man must do, which if he does not do, he must perish." That is the Arminian way of salvation. Now last week I thought of this very theory of salvation, when I stood by the side of that window of Carisbrooke Castle, out of which King Charles, of unhappy and unrighteous memory, attempted to escape. I read in the guide book that everything was provided for his escape; his followers had means at the bottom of the wall to enable him to fly across the country, and on the coast they had their boats lying ready to take him to another land; in fact, everything was ready for his escape. But here was the important circumstance: his friends had done all they could; he was to do the rest; but that doing the rest was just the point and brunt of the battle. It was to get out of the window, out of which he was not able to escape by any means, so that all his friends did for him went for nothing, so far as he was concerned. So with the sinner. If God had provided every means of escape, and only required him to get out of his dungeon, he would have remained there to all eternity. Why, is not the sinner by nature dead in sin? And if God requires him to make himself alive, and then afterwards he will do the rest for him, then verily, my friends, we are not so much obliged to God as we had thought for; for if he require so much as that of us, and we can do it, we can do the rest without his assistance. The Romanists have an extraordinary miracle of their own about St. Dennis, of whom they tell the lying legend that after his head was off he took it up in his hands and walked with it two thousand miles; whereupon said a wit, "So far as the two thousand miles go, it is nothing at all; it is only the first step in which there is any difficulty." So I believe, if that is taken, all the rest can be easily accomplished. And if God does require of the sinner—dead in sin—that he should take the first step, then he requireth just that which renders salvation as impossible under the gospel as ever it was under the law, seeing man is as unable to believe as he is to obey, and is just as much without power to come to Christ as he is without power to go to heaven without Christ. The power must be given to him of the Spirit. He lieth dead in sin; the Spirit must quicken him. He is bound hand and foot and fettered by transgression; the Spirit must cut his bonds, and then he will leap to liberty. God must come and dash the iron bars out of their sockets, and then he can escape from the window, and make good his escape afterwards; but unless the first thing be done for him, he must perish as surely under the gospel as he would have done under the law. I would cease to preach, if I believed that God, in the matter of salvation, required anything whatever of man which he himself had not also engaged to furnish. For how many have I frequently hanging upon my lips of the worst of characters—men whose lives have become so horribly bad, that the lip of morality would refuse to give a description of their character? When I enter my pulpit am I to believe that these men are to do something before God's Spirit will operate upon them? If so, I should go there with a faint heart, feeling that I never could induce them to do the first part. But now I come to my pulpit with a sure confidence—God the Holy Spirit will meet with these men this morning. They are as bad as they can be; he will put a new thought into their hearts; he will give them new wishes, he will give them new wills, and those who hated Christ will desire to love him; those who once loved sin will, by God's divine Spirit, be made to hate it; and here is my confidence, that what they cannot do, in that they are weak through the flesh, God sending his Spirit into their hearts will do for them, and in them, and so they shall be saved.

Well, then, says one, that will make people sit still and fold their arms. Sir, it will not. But if men did so I could not help it; my business, as I have often said in this place before, is not to prove to you the reasonableness of any truth, nor to defend any truth from its consequences; all I do here—and I mean to keep to it, is just to assert the truth, because it is in the Bible; then, if you do not like it, you must settle the quarrel with my Master, and if you think it unreasonable you must quarrel with the Bible. Let others defend Scripture and prove it to be true; they can do their work better than I could; mine is just the mere work of proclaiming. I am the messenger; I tell the Master's message; if you do not like the message quarrel with the Bible, not with me; so long as I have Scripture on my side I will dare and defy you to do anything against me. "Salvation is of the Lord." The Lord has to apply it, to make the unwilling willing, to make the ungodly godly, and bring the vile rebel to the feet of Jesus, or else salvation will never be accomplished. Leave that one thing undone, and you have broken the link of the chain, the very link which was just necessary to its integrity. Take away the fact that God begins the good work, and that he sends us what the old divines call preventing grace —take that away, and you have spoilt the whole of salvation; you have just taken the key-stone out of the arch, and down it tumbles. There is nothing left then.

And now on the next point we shall a little disagree again. "Salvation is of the Lord," *as to the sustaining of the work in any man's heart.* When a man is made a child of God he does not have a stock of grace given to him with which to go on for ever, but he has grace for that day; and he must have grace for the next day and grace for the next, and grace for the next, until days shall end, or else the beginning shall be of no avail. As a man does not make himself spiritually alive, so neither can he keep himself so. He can feed on spiritual food, and so preserve his spiritual strength; he can walk in the commandments of the Lord, and so enjoy rest and peace, but still the inner life is dependent upon the Spirit as much for its after existence as for its first begetting. I do verily believe that if it should ever be my lot to put my foot upon the golden threshold of paradise, and put this thumb upon the pearly latch, I should never cross the threshold unless I had grace given me to take that last step whereby I might enter heaven. No man of himself, even when converted, hath any power, except us that power is daily, constantly, and perpetually infused into him by the Spirit. But Christians often set up for independent gentlemen; they get a little stock of grace in hand, and they say, "My mountain standeth firm, I shall never be moved." But ah! it is not long before the manna begins to be putrid. It was only meant to be the manna for the day, and we have kept it for the morrow, and therefore it fails us. We must have fresh grace.

"For day by day the manna fell,
Oh to learn that lesson well."

So look day by day for fresh grace. Frequently too the Christian wants to have grace enough for a month vouchsafed to him in one moment. "Oh!" he says, "what a host of troubles I have coming—how shall I meet them all? Oh! that I had grace enough to bear me through them all!" My dear friends, you will have grace enough for your troubles, as they come one by one. "As thy days, so shall thy strength be;" but thy strength shall never be as thy months, or as thy weeks. Thou shalt have thy strength as thou hast thy bread. "Give us this day our daily bread." Give us this day our daily grace. But why is it you will get troubling yourself about the things of to-morrow? The common people say, "Cross a bridge when you come to it." That is good advice. Do the same. When a trouble comes, attack it, and down with it, and master it; but do not begin now to forestall your woes. "Ah! but I have so many" says one. Therefore I say, do not look further before thee than thou needest. "Sufficient unto the day is the *evil* thereof." Do as the brave Grecian did, who, when he defended his country from Persia, did not go into the plains to fight, but stood in the narrow pass of Thermopylæ; there, when the myriads came to him, they had to come one by one, and he felled them to the earth. Had he ventured into the plain he would have been soon devoured, and his handfull would have been melted like a drop of dew in the sea. Stand in the narrow pass of to-day, and fight thy troubles one by one; but do not rush into the plains of to-morrow, for there thou wilt be routed and killed. As the evil is sufficient so will the grace be. "Salvation is of the Lord."

But, lastly, upon this point. *The ultimate perfection of salvation is of the Lord.* Soon, soon, the saints of earth shall be saints in light; their hairs of snowy age shall be crowned with perpetual joy and everlasting youth; their eyes, suffused with tears, shall be made bright as stars, never to be clouded again by sorrow; their hearts that tremble now are to be made joyous and fast, and set for ever like pillars in the temple of God. Their follies, their burdens, their griefs, their woes, are soon to be over; sin is to be slain, corruption is to be removed, and a heaven of spotless purity and of unmingled peace is to be theirs for ever. But it must still be by grace. As was the foundation such must the top-stone be; that which laid on earth the first beginning must lay in heaven the top-most stone. As they were redeemed from their filthy conversation by grace, so they must be redeemed from death and the grave by grace too, and they must enter heaven singing,

"Salvation of the Lord alone,
Grace is a shoreless sea."

There may be Arminians here, but they will not be Arminians there; they may here say, "It is of the will of the flesh," but in heaven they shall not think so. Here they may ascribe some little to the creature; but there they shall cast their crowns at the Redeemer's feet, and acknowledge that he did it all. Here they may sometimes look a little at themselves, and boast somewhat of their own strength; but there, "Not unto us, not unto us," shall be sung with deeper sincerity and with more profound emphasis than they have ever sung it here below. In heaven, when grace shall have done its work, this truth shall stand out in blazing letters of gold, "Salvation is of the Lord."

II. Thus I have tried to expound the gospel. Now shall I show you HOW GOD HAS HEDGED THIS DOCTRINE ABOUT?

Some have said salvation in some cases is the result of *natural temperament.* Well, sir, well; God has effectually answered your argument. You say that some people are saved because they are naturally religious and inclined to be good; unfortunately I have never met with any of that class of persons yet; but I will suppose for a moment that there are such people. God has unanswerably met your objection; for, strange to say, the great number of those who are saved are just the most unlikely people in the world to have been saved while a great number of those who perish were once just the very people whom, if natural disposition had anything to do with it, we should have expected to see in heaven. Why, there is one here who in his youth was a child of many follies. Often did his mother weep over him, and cry and groan over her son's wanderings; for what with a fierce high spirit that could brook neither bit nor bridle, what with perpetual rebellions and ebullitions of hot anger, she said, " My son, my son, what wilt thou be in thy riper years ? Surely thou wilt dash in pieces law and order, and be a disgrace to thy father's name." He grew up; in youth he was wild and wanton, but, wonder of wonders, on a sudden he became a new man, changed, altogether changed; no more like what he was before than angels are like lost spirits. He sat at her feet, he cheered her heart, and the lost, fiery one became gentle, mild, humble as a little child, and obedient to God's commandments. You say, wonder of wonders ! But there is another here. He was a fair youth: when but a child he talked of Jesus; often when his mother had him on her knee he asked her questions about heaven; he was a prodigy, a wonder of piety in his youth. As he grew up, the tear rolled down his cheek under any sermon; he could scarcely bear to hear of death without a sigh; sometimes his mother caught him, as she thought, in prayer alone. And what is he now ? He has just this very morning come from sin; he has become the debauched, desperate villain, has gone far into all manner of wickedness and lust, and sin, and has become more damnably corrupt than other men could have made him; only his own evil spirit, once confined, has now developed itself, he has learned to play the lion in his manhood, as once he played the fox in his youth. I do not know whether you have ever met with such a case; but it very frequently is so. I know I can say that in my congregation some abandoned, wicked fellow, has had his heart broken, and been led to weep, and has cried to God for mercy, and renounced his vile sin; whilst some fair maiden by his side hath heard the same sermon, and if there was a tear she brushed it away; she still continues just what she was, "without God and without hope in the world." God has taken the base things of the world, and has just picked his people out of the very roughest of men, in order that he may prove, that it is not natural disposition, but that "Salvation is of the Lord " alone.

Well, but some say, it is *the minister* they hear who converts men. Ah ! that is a grand idea, full sure. No man but a fool would entertain it. I met with a man sometime ago who assured me that he knew a minister who had a very large amount of converting power in him. Speaking of a great Evangelist in America, he said, " That man, sir, has got the greatest quantity of converting power I ever knew a man to have; and Mr. So-and-so in a neighbouring town I think is second to him." At that time this converting power was being exhibited; two hundred persons were converted by the converting power of this second best, and joined to the church in a few months. I went to the place some time afterwards—it was in England—and I said, " How do your converts get on ?" " Well," said he, " I cannot say much about them." " How many out of those two hundred whom you received in a year ago stand fast ?" " Well," he said, " I am afraid not many of them; we have turned seventy of them out for drunkenness already." " Yes," I said, " I thought so: that is the end of the grand experiment of converting power." If I could convert you all, any one else might unconvert you; what any man can do another man can undo; it is only what God does that is abiding.

No, my brethren; God has taken good care it shall never be said conversion is of man, for usually he blesses those who seem to be the most unlikely to be useful. I do not expect to see so many conversions in this place as I had a year ago, when I had far fewer hearers. Do you ask why ? Why, a year ago I was abused by everybody; to mention my name was to mention the name of the most abominable buffoon that lived. The mere utterance of it brought forth oaths and cursing; with many men it was a name of contempt, kicked about the street as a foot-ball; but then God gave me souls by hundreds, who were added to my church, and in one year it was my happiness to see not less than a thousand personally who had then been converted. I do not expect that now. My name is somewhat esteemed now, and the great ones of the earth think it no dishonor to sit at my feet; but this makes me fear lest my God should forsake me now that the world esteems me. I would rather be despised and slandered than aught else. This assembly that you think so grand and fine, I would readily part with, if by such a loss I could gain a greater blessing. "God has chosen the base things of the world;" and, therefore I reckon that the more esteemed I may be the worse is my position, so much the less expectation shall I have that God will bless me. He hath put his "treasure in earthen vessels, that the excellency of the power may be of God, and not of man." A poor minister began to preach once, and all the world spoke ill of him; but God blessed him. By-and-by they turned round and petted him. He was the man—a wonder! God left him! It has often been the same. It is for us to recollect, in all times of popularity, that "Crucify him, crucify him" follows fast upon the heels of "Hosanna," and that the crowd to-day, if dealt faithfully with, may turn into the handful of to-morrow; for men love not plain speaking. We should learn to be despised, learn to be contemned, learn to be slandered, and then we shall learn to be made useful by God. Down on my knees have I often fallen, with the hot sweat rising from my brow, under some fresh slander poured upon me; in an agony of grief my heart has been well-nigh broken; till at last I learned the art of bearing all and caring for none. And now my grief runneth in another line. It is just the opposite. I fear lest God should forsake me, to prove that he is the author of salvation—that it is not in the preacher, that it is not in the crowd, that it is not in the attention I can attract, but in God, and in God alone. And this thing I hope I can say from my heart: If to be made as the mire of the streets again, if to be the laughing stock of fools and the song of the drunkard once more will make me more serviceable to my Master, and more useful to his cause, I will prefer it to all this multitude, or to all the applause that man could give. Pray for me, dear friends, pray for me, that God would still make me the means of the salvation of souls; for I fear he may say, "I will not help that man, lest the world should say he has done it, for "salvation is of the Lord," and so it must be, even to the world's end.

III. And now WHAT IS, WHAT SHOULD BE, THE INFLUENCE OF THIS DOCTRINE UPON MEN?

Why, first, with sinners, this doctrine is *a great battering-ram against their pride.* I will give you a figure. The sinner in his natural estate reminds me of a man who has a strong and well-nigh impenetrable castle into which he has fled. There is the outer moat; there is a second moat; there are the high walls; and then afterwards there is the dungeon and keep, into which the sinner will retire. Now, the first moat that goes round the sinner's trusting place is his good works. "Ah!" he says, "I am as good as my neighbour; twenty shillings in the pound down, ready money, I have always paid; I am no sinner; 'I title mint and cummin;' a good respectable gentlemen I am indeed." Well, when God comes to work with him, to save him, he sends his army across the first moat; and as they go through it, they cry, "Salvation is of the Lord;" and the moat is dried up, for if it be of the Lord, how can it be of good works? But when that is done, he has a second intrenchment—ceremonies. "Well," he says, "I will not trust in my good works, but I have been baptized, I have been confirmed; do not I take the sacrament? That shall be my trust," "Over the moat! Over the moat!" And the soldiers go over again, shouting, "Salvation is of the Lord." The second moat is dried up; it is all over with that. Now they come to the first strong wall; the sinner, looking over it, says, "I can repent, I can believe, whenever I like; I will save myself by repenting and believing." Up come the soldiers of God, his great army of conviction, and they batter this wall to the ground, crying, "'Salvation is of the Lord.' Your faith and your repentance must all be given you, or else you will neither believe nor repent of sin." And now the castle is taken; the man's hopes are all cut off; he feels that it is not of self; the castle of self is overcome, and the great banner upon which is written "Salvation is of the Lord" is displayed upon the battlements. But is the battle over? Oh no; the sinner has retired to the keep, in the centre of the castle; and now he changes his tactics. "I cannot save myself," says he, "therefore I will despair; there is no salvation for me." Now this second castle is as hard to take as the first, for the sinner sits down and says, "I can't be saved, I must perish." But God commands the soldiers to take this castle too, shouting, "Salvation *is* of the Lord;" though it is not of man, *it is of God;* "he is able to save, even to the uttermost," though you cannot save yourself. This sword, you see, cuts two ways; it cuts pride down, and then it cleaves the skull of despair. If any man say he can save himself, it halveth his pride at once; and if another man say he cannot be saved, it dasheth his despair to the earth; for it affirms that he can be saved, seeing, "Salvation *is* of the Lord." That is the effect this doctrine has upon the sinner: may it have that effect on you!

But what influence has it upon the saint? Why, it is the keystone of all divinity. *I will defy you to be heterodox* if you believe this truth. You must be sound in the faith if you have learned to spell this sentence—"Salvation is of the Lord;" and if you feel it in your soul *you will not be proud;* you cannot be; you will cast everything at his feet, confessing that you have done nothing, save what he has helped you to do; and therefore the glory must be where the salvation is. If you believe this *you will not be distrustful.* You will say, "My salvation does not depend on my faith, but on the Lord; my keeping does not depend on myself, but on God who keepeth me; my being brought to heaven rests not now in my own hands, but in the hands of God; you will, when doubts and fears prevail, fold your arms, look upwards, and say,

> "And now my eye of faith is dim,
> I trust in Jesus, sink or swim."

If you can keep this in your mind *you may always be joyful.* He can have no cause for trouble who knows and feels that his salvation is of God. Come on, legions of hell; come on, demons of the pit!

> "He that has helped me bears me through,
> And makes me more than conqueror too,"

Salvation resteth not on this poor arm, else should I despair, but on the arm of yon Omnipotent—that arm on which the pillars of the heavens do lean. "Whom should I fear? The Lord is my strength and my life; of whom shall I be afraid?" And this, may by grace, *nerve you to work for God.* If you had to save your neighbours you might sit down and do nothing; but since "Salvation is of the Lord," go on and prosper. Go and preach the gospel; go and tell the gospel everywhere. Tell it in your house, tell it in the street, tell it in every land and every nation; for it is not of yourself, it is "of the Lord." Why do not our friends go to Ireland to preach the gospel? Ireland is a disgrace to the Protestant church. Why do not they go and preach there? A year or so ago a number of our brave ministers went over there to preach; they did right bravely; they went there, and they came back again, and that is about the sum total of the glorious expedition against Popery. But why come back again? Because they were stoned, good easy men! Do they not think that the gospel ever will spread without a few stones? But they would have been killed! Brave martyrs they! Let them be enrolled in the red chronicle. Did the martyrs of old, did the apostles, shrink from going to any country because they would have been killed? No, they were ready to die; and if half a dozen ministers had been killed in Ireland, it would have been the finest thing in the world for liberty in future; for after that the people dare not have touched us; the strong arm of the law would have put them down; we might have gone through every village of Ireland afterwards, and been at peace; the constabulary would soon have put an end to such infamous murder; it would have awakened the Protestantism of England to claim the liberty which is our right there as we give it elsewhere. We shall never see any great change till we have some men in our ranks who are willing to be martyrs. That deep ditch can never be crossed till the bodies of a few of us shall fill it up; and after that it will be easy work to preach the gospel there. Our brethren should go there once more. They can leave their white cravats at home, and the white feather too, and go forth with a brave heart and a bold spirit; and if the people mock and scoff, let them mock and scoff on. George Whitfield said, when he preached on Kennington Common, where they threw dead cats and rotten eggs at him, "This is only the manure of Methodism, the best thing in the world to make it grow; throw away as fast as you please." And when a stone cut him on the forehead, he seemed to preach the better for a little blood-letting. Oh for such a man to dare the mob, and then the mob would not need to be dared. Let us go there, recollecting that "Salvation is of the Lord," and let us in every place and at every time preach God's Word, believing that God's Word is more than a match for man's sin, and God will yet be master over all the earth.

My voice fails me again, and my thoughts too. I was weary this morning, when I came into this pulpit, and I am weary now. Sometimes I am joyous and glad, and feel in the pulpit as if I could preach for ever; at other times I feel glad to close; but yet with such a text I would that I could have finished up with all the might that mortal lip could summon. Oh! to let men know this, that their salvation is of God! Swearer, swear not against him in whose hand thy breath is! Despiser, despise not him who can save you or destroy you. And thou hypocrite, seek not to deceive him from whom salvation comes, and who therefore knows right well whether thy salvation has come from him.

IV. And now in concluding let me just tell you WHAT IS THE OBVERSE OF THIS TRUTH. Salvation is of God: then *damnation is of man.* If any of you are damned, you will have no one to blame but yourselves; if any of you perish, the blame will not lie at God's door; if you are lost and cast away, you will have to bear all the blame and all the tortures of conscience yourself; you will lie for ever in perdition, and reflect, " I have destroyed myself; I have made a suicide of my soul; I have been my own destroyer; I can lay no blame to God." Remember, if saved, you must be saved by God alone, though if lost you have lost yourselves. "Turn ye, turn ye, why will ye die O house of Israel." With my last faltering sentence I bid you stop and think. Ah! my hearers, my hearers! it is an awful thing to preach to such a mass as this. But the other Sunday, as I came down stairs, I was struck with a memorable sentence, uttered by one who stood there. He said, " There are 8000 people this morning without excuse in the day of judgment." I should like to preach so that this always might be said; and if I cannot, O may God have mercy on me, for his name's sake! But now remember! Ye have souls; those souls will be damned, or saved. Which will it be ? Damned they must be for ever, unless God shall save you; unless Christ shall have mercy upon you, there is no hope for you. Down on your knees! Cry to God for mercy. Now lift up your heart in prayer to God. May now be the very time when you shall be saved. Or ever the next drop of blood shall run through your veins, may you find peace! Remember, that peace is to be had now. If you feel now your need of it, it is to be had now. And how? For the mere asking for it. "Ask, and it shall be given you; seek, and ye shall find."

> " But if your ears refuse
>   The language of his grace,
> Your hearts grow hard, like stubborn Jews,
>   That unbelieving race,
>
> The Lord with vengeance drest,
>   Shall lift his hand and swear,
> You that despise my promis'd rest
>   Shall have no portion there."

Oh that ye may not be despisers, lest ye " wonder and perish!" May ye now fly to Christ, and be accepted in the beloved. It is my last best prayer. May the Lord hear it! Amen.

Things that Accompany Salvation

"Things that accompany Salvation."—Hebrews vi. 9.

I AM not quite certain that my text will warrant all I shall say upon it this day, if read and understood in its connection. But I have taken the words rather by accommodation than otherwise, and shall make use of them as a kind of heading to the discourse which I hope to be enabled to deliver. I sat myself down, and I meditated on this subject—" Things that accompany Salvation." And after some period of rumination, my thoughts assumed the form of an allegory ; in which I hope to present them to you this morning. I compared Salvation to a rich and costly treasure, which God in his infinite love and mercy had determined to send into the world; and I remembered that our Lord Jesus was so much interested in the bringing of this Salvation to this earth, that he did send all that he had, and came himself to attend and to accompany this Salvation. I then pictured to myself a great march of bright ones through this land, carrying in their midst the sacred jewel of Salvation. I looked forward, and I saw a mighty van-guard, who already had attained the shores of Eternity. I looked around Salvation, and I saw it always in every case attended with divers graces and virtues which seemed to be like troops and soldiers to guard it in the van, about its flanks, and in the rear.

Before we begin, however, let us just make this caution. When the Apostle speaks of virtues and of graces, he calls them " things that accompany Salvation," not things which cause it. Our faith does not cause Salvation, nor our hope, nor our love, nor our good works; they are things which attend it as its guard of honor. The origin of Salvation lies alone in the sovereign will of God the Father ; in the infinite efficacy of the blood of Jesus—God the Son; and in the divine influence of God the Holy Spirit. There are, however, " things that accompany Salvation." Picture then to yourselves the march of some ancient monarch through his territory. We read stories of eastern monarchs in the olden time, that seem more like romance than reality; when they marched with thousands of flying banners, and with all kinds of riches borne with them. Now you are to take that as the basis of my figure, and suppose Salvation to be the sacred treasure which is being carried through the world, with guards before and guards behind, to accompany it on its journey.

We will begin, then, with *the advance-guard that has accompanied Salvation* or rather *gone before it.* We shall then come to *those who immediately precede it,* and then we shall notice *those who accompany it by its side,* and conclude by noticing *the rear guard attending upon this Salvation of our God.*

I. First, then, IN THE MARCHES OF TROOPS AND ARMIES, THERE ARE SOME THAT ARE OUTRIDERS, AND GO FAR AHEAD OF THE OTHER TROOPS." So in the march of Salvation," which have far preceded it to clear the way. I will tell you the names of these stupendous Titans who have gone before. The first is *Election ;* the second is *Predestination ;* the third is *Redemption ;* and the *Covenant* is the captain of them all. Before Salvation came into this world, Election marched in the very forefront, and it had for its work the billeting of Salvation. Election went through the world and marked the houses to which Salvation should come and the hearts in which the treasure should be deposited. Election looked through all the race of man, from Adam down to the last, and marked with sacred stamp those for whom Salvation was designed. "He must needs go through Samaria," said Election ; and Salvation must go there. Then came Predestination. Predestination did not merely mark the house, but it mapped the road in which Salvation should travel to that house; Predestination ordained every step of the great army of Salvation; it ordained the time when the sinner should be brought to Christ, the manner how he should be saved, the means that should be employed; it marked the exact hour and moment, when God the Spirit should quicken the dead in sin, and when peace and pardon should be spoken through the blood of Jesus. Predestination marked the way so completely, that Salvation doth never overstep the bounds, and it is never at a loss for the road. In the everlasting decree of the Sovereign God, the footsteps of Mercy were every one of them ordained. As nothing in this world revolves by chance—as even the foreknown station of a rush by the river is as fixed as the station of a king—it was not meet that Salvation should be left to chance; and therefore God has mapped the place where it should pitch its tent, the manner of its footsteps to that tent, and the time when it should arrive there. Then came Redemption. The way was rough; and though Election had marked the house, and Predestination had mapped the road, the way was so impeded that Salvation could not travel it until it had been cleared. Forth came Redemption; it had but one weapon ; that weapon was the all-victorious cross of Christ. There stood the mountains of our sins; Redemption smote them, and they split in halves and left a valley for the Lord's redeemed to march through. There was the great gulph of God's offended wrath; Redemption bridged it with the cross, and so left an everlasting passage by which the armies of the Lord may cross. Redemption has tunnelled every mountain; it has dried up every sea, cut down every forest; it has levelled every high hill, and filled up the valleys, so that the road of Salvation is now plain and simple. God can be just, and yet the justifier of the ungodly.

Now, this sacred advance-guard carry for their banner the Eternal Covenant. Election, Predestination, and Redemption—the things that have gone before, beyond the sight, are all rallied to the battle by this standard—the Covenant, the Everlasting Covenant, ordered in all things and sure. We know and believe that before the morning star startled the shades of darkness, God had covenanted with his Son that he should die and pay a ransom price, and that, on God the Father's part, he would give to Jesus "a number whom no man could number," who should be purchased by his blood, and through that blood should be most securely saved. Now, when Election marches forward, it carries the Covenant. These are chosen in the Covenant of grace. When Predestination marcheth, and when it marketh out the way of Salvation, it proclaims the Covenant. "He marked out the places of the people according to the tribes of Israel." And Redemption also, pointing to the precious blood of Christ, claims Salvation for the blood-bought ones, because the Covenant hath decreed it to to be theirs.

Now, my dear hearers, this advance-guard is so far ahead that you and I cannot see them. These are true doctrines, but very mysterious; they are beyond our sight; and if we wish to see Salvation, we must not stop until we see the van-guard, because they are so far off that only the eye of faith can reach them. We must have that sacred glass, that divine telescope of faith, or else we shall never have the evidence of things not seen. Let us rest certain, however, that if we have Salvation we have Election. He that believeth is elected; whoever casts himself on Christ as a guilty sinner, is certainly God's chosen child. As sure as ever you believe on the Saviour, and go to him, you were predestinated to do so from all eternity, and your faith is the great mark and evidence that you are chosen of God, and precious in his esteem. Dost thou believe? Then Election is thine. Dost thou believe? Then Predestination is as surely thine as thou art alive. Dost thou trust alone in Jesus? Then fear not; Redemption was meant for thee. So then, we will not be struck with terror at that grand advance-guard that hath already gained the celestial hill, and have prepared the place where the elect shall for ever repose upon the bosom of their God.

II. But mark, we are about to review THE ARMY THAT IMMEDIATELY PRECEDES SALVATION; and first, in the forefront of these, there marches one whose name we must pronounce with sacred awe. It is God, the Holy Spirit. Before anything can be done in our salvation, there must come that Third Person of the Sacred Trinity. Without him, faith, repentance, humility, love, are things quite impossible. Even the blood of our Lord Jesus Christ cannot save until it has been applied to the heart by God the Holy Spirit. Before we notice the grand army, then, that immediately precedes Salvation, let us be cautious that we do not forget Him who is the leader of them all. The great King, immortal, invisible, the Divine person, called the Holy Ghost, the Holy Spirit: it is he that quickens the soul, or else it would lie dead for ever; it is he that makes it tender, or else it would never feel; it is he that imparts efficacy to the Word preached, or else it could never reach further than the ear; it is he who breaks the heart, it is he who makes it whole: he, from first to last, is the great worker of Salvation in us, just as Jesus Christ was the author of Salvation for us. O soul, by this mayest thou know whether Salvation has come to thine house—art thou a partaker of the Holy Spirit? Come now, answer thou this question—hath he ever breathed on thee? Hath he ever breathed into thee? Canst thou say that thou hast been the subject of his supernatural influence? For, if not, remember except a man be born of the Spirit from above, he cannot see the kingdom of God. That which is born of the flesh is flesh; only that which is born of the Spirit is spirit. Thy best exertions will be all unavailing unless the Holy Ghost shall work in thee, to will and to do of God's good pleasure. The highest efforts of the flesh can never reach higher than the flesh, just as water of itself will never run higher than its source. You may be moral, you may be strictly upright, you may be much that is commendable; but unless you be partakers of the Holy Spirit, Salvation is as impossible to you as it is even to the lost. We must be born again, and born again by that divine influence; or else it is all in vain. Remember, then, that the Spirit of God always accompanies Salvation.

And now, close in the rear of the adorable Spirit follow the Thundering Legion. No sooner does God the Holy Ghost come into the soul, than he brings with him what I have called the Thundering Legion; and those of you that have been saved will not be at a loss to understand what I mean. This Thundering Legion are clad in mail; their helmets wave with horror; their speech is rough like men that come from a far country; their faces are terrible to look upon, for they are like unto lions, and do terribly affright the timid. Some of the men in this Thundering Legion bear with them swords; with these swords they are to slay the sinner. For, before he can be made whole, he must be spiritually killed; the sword must pierce him, and must slay all his selfishness before he can be brought to the Lord Jesus. Then another body of them carry with them axes, with which they cut down the thick trees of our pride and abase the goodly cedars of our righteousness. There are with them those that fill up the wells with stones, and break up all the cisterns of our carnal sufficiency, until we are driven to despair, having all our hopes despoiled. Then come those who, with brazen trumpets, or with trumps of rams horns—like those who once razed Jericho level with the ground—do blow a blast, so shrill and dread, that the sinner thinks that even the yells of hell itself could not be more terrible. Then come those who with lances pierce the spirit through and through; and in the rear are the ten great guns, the artillery of the law, which perpetually fire upon the wounded spirit till it knows not what it is, nor what it does. My friend, has this Thundering Legion ever come to your house? Have they ever taken up their quarters in your heart? For, rest assured, these are some of the "things that accompany Salvation." What I have said is no allegory to those who have been converted, but it may be a mystery to those who know not the Lord. Understand, then, that the first work of God the Spirit in the soul is a terrible work. Before a man can be truly converted, he must suffer great agony of spirit; all our self-righteousness must be laid level with the ground, and trampled like the miry streets. Our carnal hopes must, every one of them, be cut in pieces, and our refuges of lies must be swept away with the hail of God's anger. The law of God will appear terrible to the sinner when he is first convinced of sin. "What have I done?" he will say. Or rather, "What have I undone? I have undone myself." See him when God the Spirit has first convinced him of sin; you would think him mad; he is thought to be mad by his worldly companions. He weeps day and night, tears become his meat and his drink; he can scarcely sleep for the dreams of hell, and when he wakes he thinks he feels it already. "Oh, the wrath to come, the wrath to come, the wrath to come!" that seems to be ever pressing on his heart. He is like John Bunyan's pilgrim, he has a heavy burden on his back, and he knows not how to get rid of it; he wrings his hands and cries, "What shall I do? I am undone. I have rebelled against God, and God is angry with me." Ah, I tell you this Thundering Legion is a terrible thing indeed. God be praised, when once they go out of the heart there is some joy; but whilst they are billited in the conscience of man, I defy him to eat or drink with any mirth or joy. The poor town of Mansoul is hung with black all the time these rough soldiers are there. Hideous threatenings and doleful forebodings are the sinner's only company in such a case. He seeks to find a little hope and comfort in his own doings; down comes the hammer of the Law, and breaks all his doings to pieces. He thinks, well he will rest on the couch of Indifference and Sloth; forth comes the Law, ties him to the halberts, takes its ten-thonged whip and begins to lay on to him with all his might till his heart bleeds again. Then comes Conscience with its brine, and washes him all over; and he is exceedingly tormented, for even his bed is become a bed of spikes and thorns. This Thundering Legion always precedes Salvation. More or less of terrors every man must feel before he is converted. Some have less, some have more; but there must be some measure of this terrible law work in the soul, or else Salvation is not come to a man's house.

Oh, Thundering Legion, ye are gone; we hear their trumpets and the dying echoes still appal us. We can remember, brethren, those terrible days when they were in our house and in our heart. They are gone. What see we in the rear of them? Close in the rear there follows a broken heart. Look at it; do not despise it; God never despises it; do not thou. "A broken and a contrite heart O God, thou wilt not despise." I see how this poor broken heart is broken; it is rent to its very core and centre; it is bathed in tears; it is overwhelmed with suffering. See its humility; it never talks about boasting now. Mark its repentance; the sins it loved before it hates now; it speaks not about self-salvation. Hear it, as the broken heart speaks out its broken language. Hear it—"Lord have mercy upon me a sinner!" Do not fear to come and look at this broken heart; how sweetly is it perfumed! The sacred smell of a sacrifice which God approves rises from it. Hear it, as again it speaks—"Lord, save, or I perish." See this poor broken heart when it is in the world and at its business; it interrupts its business with ejaculations like these—" Oh that—Ah, ah—would that!" And when it can get alone, it pours out its heart before God, and cries,

> Unclean, unclean, and full of sin
> From first to last, O Lord I've been;
> Deceitful is my heart.'

Oh wash my soul in Jesus' blood; forgive me all my guilt, and I will be thy servant for ever and ever.

Dear hearers, has this broken heart ever come to your house? Rest assured I am speaking God's own truth, that admits of no dispute—unless this broken heart has come within your bosom you cannot be made partakers of Christ. The heart must first be pounded in the mortar of conviction, and beaten in pieces with the pestle of the law, or else it never can receive the grace of the Comforter in all its plenitude. Are you broken-hearted to-day? Are you sorrowful at this very hour? Be of good cheer, Salvation is not far behind. When there is once a broken heart, there is mercy very near. The broken heart is the prelude of healing. He that kills will make whole; he that woundeth will bind up; he that smote will cure. God is looking on thee with love, and will have mercy upon thee.

But who are those that follow in the rear? Another troop, another legion; but these are far different from the rest. The silken legion follow; these are not clad in steel; they have no helmets of war upon their head; they have smiling looks and countenances that are full of joy. No weapons of war in their hands; no thunders do they utter; but they speak kind words of pity, and their hands are full of benedictions. Shall I tell you who this silken legion are? There is a troop of them who take the poor wounded heart, and wash it first in blood; they sprinkle on it the sacred blood of the Atonement; and it is amazing how the poor broken heart, though faint and sick, revives at the first drop of the precious blood of our Lord Jesus Christ; and when well washed in blood, another of this legion steps forward and takes it and washes it in water—for both water and blood flowed from the Saviour's heart.

> " Let the water and the blood,
> From thy wounded side which flow'd
> Be of sin the double cure,
> Cleanse me from its guilt and power."

And oh, what a washing it is! The heart that was once black as the coals of hell, seems white as the snow of Lebanon. When it has once been bathed in the bath of the Saviour's blood and water, oh, how pure it becomes! He who was black as the tents of Kedar becomes fair as the curtains of Solomon. Then follow those who pour oil and wine into the wounds of this poor broken heart, so that where it smarted before, the wounds begin to sing. The sacred oil and wine of the precious promise is poured into every wound; and then follow those who with downy fingers bind up the heart with the sacred liniment of Promise till it seems no longer broken, but the broken heart rejoices. The whole heart sings for gladness; for God hath restored its strength and bound up all its wounds, according to his promise: "He healeth the broken in heart, and bindeth up their wounds." And then, since the work is not quite done, there come those who carry the King's wardrobe; and with the things out of this rich storehouse they array the soul from head to foot; they clothe it with everything that for lustre and for glory could adorn it, and make it bright as the spirits before the throne. And then the King's jewellers come in and complete the whole; they array the soul with ornaments, and bedeck it with precious stones. As the Father said, "Bring forth the best robe and put it on him, and put a ring on his hand and shoes on his feet," even so do this Silken Legion wash and heal and cleanse and glorify the once poor broken heart. Have these ever come to your house? It is an allegory, but it is all plair to him that understandeth it. Sinner, hast thou ever had the blood of Christ applied to thee?

> " Couldst thou look and see the flowing
> Of his soul's redeeming blood,
> With divine assurance knowing
> He hath made thy peace with God?"

Dost thou this hour lay thine hand on the dear head of Christ; confess thy sin, and believe that he was punished for thee? Thou canst? Then, verily salvation is thine. And has thine heart been ever washed with water? Say, dost thou hate sin? Is thy guilt all cleansed, and is the power of guilt cut away, so that thou dost not love the ways of iniquity, nor seek to run in the paths of transgressors? Then thou art an heir of heaven. And say, poor sinner, hast thou ever been arrayed in the robe of Jesus' righteousness? Couldst thou ever fondly hope that thou wast accepted in the Beloved? Methinks I see thee with the tear in thine eye, and hear thee saying, I have sometimes sung with all my heart—

> " Jesus, thy blood and righteousness
> My beauty are, my glorious dress;
> 'Midst flaming worlds, in these array'd,
> With joy shall I lift my head.
>
> Bold shall I stand in that great day,
> For who aught to my charge shall lay?
> Fully absolved through Christ I am
> From sin's tremendous curse and shame."

And now we have not yet come to a full conviction of Salvation. The Silken Legion are gone; their banners are still flying in the gale, and their trumpets of promise are still making the air glad with melody. What cometh next? Now come those that are the actual attendants upon Salvation—or rather, that march in the rank immediately before it. There are four of these, called *Repentance, Humility, Prayer,* and *a tender Conscience.* Just before the full assurance of Salvation there marches *Humility.* She is of a downcast look; she is not sad, but she hath no high looks; she scarcely dares to lift her eye to the place where God's honor dwelleth. She is often looking downwards, remembering her past estate; thinking of all the bitterness and the guilt of her previous life. She never boasts of what God has done for her, she looks to the hole of the pit and the miry clay from whence she was digged. She knows she has been washed in the blood of the Saviour, but she remembers how black she was before she was washed; and oh, she laments the past although she rejoices in the present. She feels her own weakness; she dares not stand alone; she leans on the arm of her Beloved; for she knows that she should fall to the ground unless he should constantly maintain her. Side by side with her, is her sister called *Repentance*, watering the ground with tears to lay the dust before the King. Wherever she goes she weeps, and if you ask her why, she will tell you she does not weep because of a fear of hell—that is all gone. The Silken Legion yonder, she tells you, have wiped all her fears away; but she weeps because she smote the Lord that loved her so well; she beats her breast, and cries—

> "'Twas you, my sins, my cruel sins,
>   His chief tormentors were;
> Each of my crimes became a nail,
>   And unbelief the spear."

The more you tell her of her Salvation, the more she weeps to think she could have rebelled against such a Saviour. She is confident that her sins are blotted out; she knows her Master has forgiven her; but she never will forgive herself. Then side by side with Repentance is one called *Prayer*. He is a priest, and he waves in his hand a censer full of odoriferous incense, that the way for the King may be prepared ; that wherever he marches there may be a sweet perfume. Prayer riseth by midnight to call upon God; its waking eyes salute the rising sun, that it may lift up its heart to Jehovah; and when the sun is setting, Prayer will not let his wheel be hidden beneath the horizon, until in his chariot he hath carried supplication. Then in this company is the fourth of those immediately attending upon Salvation, *a tender Conscience*. This tender Conscience is afraid to put one foot before the other, lest it should put its foot in the wrong place. Poor tender Conscience; some despise him; but he is dear to the King's heart. I would to God, my brethren, you and I knew more about him. I used to know a conscience so tender, that I would wish to feel it again. Then we questioned the lawfulness of every act before we committed it; and then, though it was lawful, we would stop to see if it were expedient; and if we thought it expedient, even then we would not do it, except we felt it would be abundantly honorable to the Lord our God. Every doctrine we used to scruple at, lest we should believe a lie; every ordinance we examined, lest we should commit idolatry; happy were the days when tender Conscience went with us. And now, my hearers, do you know anything about these four? Has *Humility* ever come to you? Has she ever abased your pride, and taught you to lie in the dust before God? Has *Repentance* ever watered the floor of your hearts with tears? Have you ever been led to weep in secret for your-sins, and to bewail your iniquities? Has *Prayer* ever entered your spirit? Remember, a prayerless soul is a Christless soul. Have you learned to pray, not with the parrot's cry, but with the heart's ever fresh expression. Have you ever learned to pray? And lastly are you *tender of Conscience*, for unless your conscience is made tender, salvation has not met you, for these are the immediate attendants upon it.

III. And now comes SALVATION IN ALL ITS FULNESS. The "things that accompany Salvation" make a glorious march in the forefront of it—from Election down to these precious opening buds of virtue in the sinner's heart. What a goodly array ! Sure the angels do sometimes fly along in admiration, and see this long array that heralds Salvation to the heart. And now comes the precious casket set with gems and jewels. It is of God-like workmanship; no hammer was ever lifted on it; it was smitten out and fashioned upon the anvil of Eternal Might, and cast in the mould of Everlasting Wisdom; but no human hand hath ever defiled it, and it is set with jewels so unutterably precious, that if heaven and earth were sold they could never buy another Salvation ! And who are those that are close around it? There are three sweet sisters that always have the custody of the treasure—you know them; their names are common in Scripture—Faith, Hope, and Love, the three divine sisters; these have Salvation in their bowels and do carry it about with them in their loins. *Faith*, who layeth hold on Christ, and trusteth all in him; that ventureth everything upon his blood and sacrifice, and hath no other trust. *Hope*, that with beaming eye looks up to Jesus Christ in glory, and expects him soon to come: looks downward, and when she sees grim Death in her way, expects that she shall pass through with victory. And thou sweet *Love*, the sweetest of the three; she, whose words are music and whose eyes are stars; Love, also looks to Christ and is enamoured of him; loves him in all his offices, adores his presence, reverences his words; and is prepared to bind her body to the stake and die for him, who bound his body to the cross to die for her. Sweet Love, God hath well chosen to commit to thee the custody of the sacred work. Faith, Hope, and Love—say sinner, hast thou these three? Dost thou believe that Jesus is the Son of God? Dost thou hope that through the efficacy of his merits thou shalt see thy Maker's face with joy? Dost thou love him? Say, couldst thou repeat after me,

> "Jesus! I love thy charming name,
> 'Tis music to my ear;
> Fain would I sound it out so loud
> That earth and heaven might hear.
>
> Yes, thou art precious to my soul,
> My transport and my trust;
> Jewels to thee are gaudy toys,
> And gold is sordid dust."

Have you these three graces? If so, you have Salvation. Having that, you are rich to all intents of bliss; for God in the Covenant is yours. Cast your eye forward; remember Election is yours, Predestination and Sovereign Decree are both yours; remember, the terrors of the law are past; the broken heart is mourning; the comforts of religion you have already received; the spiritual graces are already in the bud; you are an heir of immortality, and for you there is a glorious future. These are the "things that accompany Salvation."

IV. Now you must have patience with me for just a few more minutes; I MUST BRING UP THE REAR GUARD. It is impossible that with such a van guard, grace should be unattended from behind. Now see those that follow Salvation. As there were fair bright cherubs that walked in front of it—you remember still their names—Humility, Repentance, Prayer, and a tender Conscience—there are four that follow it, and march in solemn pomp into the sinner's heart. The first of these is Gratitude—always singing, "Bless the Lord O my soul, and all that is within me bless his holy name." And then Gratitude lays hold upon its son's hand; the name of that son is Obedience. "O my master," saith the heart, "thou hast done so much for me; I will obey thee"—

> "Help me to run in thy commands,
> 'Tis a delightful road;
> Nor let my heart, nor hands, nor feet,
> Offend against my God."

In company with this fair grace is one called Consecration—a pure white spirit that hath no earthliness; from its head to its foot it is all God's, and all gold. Hear it speak—

> "All that I am and all I have
> Shall be for ever thine;
> Whate'er my duty bids me give,
> My cheerful hands resign.
>
> And if I might make some reserve,
> And duty did not call,
> I love my God with zeal so great,
> That I would give him all."

Linked to this bright one, is one with a face serene and solemn, called Knowledge.

" Then shall ye know when ye follow on to know the Lord." Those that are saved understand mysteries, they know the love of Christ; they "know him, whom to know is life eternal."

Now, have you these four? They are rather the successors of Salvation than the heralds of it. "Oh yes," the believer can say, "I trust I have Gratitude, Obedience, Consecration, and Knowledge." I will not weary you, but there are three shining ones that follow after these four, and I must not forget them, for they are the flower of them all. There is Zeal with eyes of fire, and heart of flame, a tongue that burneth, a hand that never wearies, and limbs that never tire; Zeal, that flies round the world with wings swifter than the lightning's flash, and finds even then her wings too tardy for her wish. Zeal, ever ready to obey, resigning up itself for Christ, jealously affected always in a good thing. This Zeal always dwells near one that is called Communion. This, sure, is the goodliest of all the train; an angel spiritualised, an angel purified and made yet more angelic, is Communion. Communion calls in secret on its God; its God in secret sees. It is conformed to the image of Jesus; walks according to his footsteps, and lays its head perpetually on his bosom. And as a necessary consequence, on the other side of Communion—which with one hand lays hold of Zeal, is Joy—joy in the Spirit. Joy, that hath an eye more flashing than the world's merriment ever gave to mortal beauty, with light foot trips over hills of sorrow, singing in the roughest ways, of faithfulness and love. Joy, like the nightingale, sings in the dark, and can praise God in the tempest and shout his high praises in the storm. This is indeed a fitting cherub to be in the rear of Salvation. Do not forget these other three; they are after works of the Spirit, they are high attainments—Zeal, Communion, and Joy.

Now I have almost done. Just in the rear is Perseverance, final, certain and sure. Then there follows complete Sanctification, whereby the soul is purged from every sin, and made as white and pure as God himself. Now we have come to the very rear of the army; but remember as there was an advance guard so far ahead that we could not see them, so there is a rear guard so far behind that we cannot behold them now. Let us just try to see them with the eye of faith. We have seen the army; we have traced it from the Thundering Legion, guided by the Holy Spirit, till we have finished it by complete Sanctification. Hark, I hear the silver trumpet sound; there is a glorious array behind. A guard, far, far back are coming following the steps of the conquering heroes, that have already swept our sins away. Do you not see in the fore part there is one, whom men paint a skeleton. Look at him; he is not the King's terrors. I know thee, Death, I know thee. Miserably men have belied thee. Thou art no spectre; thine hand bears no dart; thou art not gaunt and frightful. I know thee, thou bright cherub: thou hast not in thy hand a dart, but a golden key that unlocks the gates of Paradise. Thou art fair to look upon, thy wings are like the wings of doves, covered with silver and like yellow gold. Behold this angel Death, and his successor Resurrection. I see three bright things coming; one is called Confidence, see it! it looks at Death; no fear is in its eye, no palor on its brow. See holy Confidence marches with steady steps; the cold chill stream of Death doth not freeze its blood. See behind it its brother Victory; hear him, as he cries, "O Death, where is thy sting? O Grave where is thy victory?"The last word, " victory," is drowned amidst *the shouts of angels.* These bring up the rear. Angels bear the spirits of the redeemed into the bosom of the Saviour—

> "Far from a world of grief and sin,
> With God eternally shut in,
> They are for ever blest."

And now follow everlasting songs—" Praise him, praise him, King of kings and Lord of lords; he hath gotten him the victory. Hallelujah, hallelujah, hallelujah, world without end!" Hallelujah, yet again!" Let the echoes of eternity perpetually cry, " Hallelujah! for

THINGS THAT ACCOMPANY YOUR SALVATION."

Salvation by Knowing the Truth

"God our Saviour; who will have all men to be saved, and to come unto the knowledge of the truth."—1 Timothy ii. 3, 4.

MAY God the Holy Ghost guide our meditations to the best practical result this evening, that sinners may be saved and saints stirred up to diligence.

I do not intend to treat my text controversially. It is like the stone which makes the corner of a building, and it looks towards a different side of the gospel from that which is mostly before us. Two sides of the building of truth meet here. In many a village there is a corner where the idle and the quarrelsome gather together; and theology has such corners. It would be very easy indeed to set ourselves in battle array, and during the next half-hour to carry on a very fierce attack against those who differ from us in opinion upon points which could be raised from this text. I do not see that any good would come of it, and, as we have very little time to spare, and life is short, we had better spend it upon something that may better tend to our edification. May the good Spirit preserve us from a contentious spirit, and help us really to profit by his word.

It is quite certain that when we read that God will have all men to be saved it does not mean that he wills it with the force of a decree or a divine purpose, for, if he did, then all men would be saved. He willed to make the world, and the world was made: he does not so will the salvation of all men, for we know that all men will not be saved. Terrible as the truth is, yet is it certain from holy writ that there are men who, in consequence of their sin and their rejection of the Saviour, will go away into everlasting punishment, where shall be weeping and wailing and gnashing of teeth. There will at the last be goats upon the left hand as well as sheep on the right, tares to be burned as well as wheat to be garnered, chaff to be blown away as well as corn to be preserved. There will be a dreadful hell as well as a glorious heaven, and there is no decree to the contrary.

What then? Shall we try to put another meaning into the text than that which it fairly bears? I trow not. You must, most of you, be acquainted with the general method in which our older Calvinistic friends deal with this text. "All men," say they,—"that is, *some men*": as if the Holy Ghost could not have said "some men" if he had meant some men. "All men," say they; "that is, some of all sorts of men": as if the Lord could not have said "all sorts of men" if he had meant that. The Holy Ghost by the apostle has written "all men," and unquestionably he means all men. I know how to get rid of the force of the "alls" according to that critical method which some time ago was very current, but I do not see how it can be applied here with due regard to truth. I was reading just now the exposition of a very able doctor who explains the text so as to explain it away; he applies grammatical gunpowder to it, and explodes it by way of expounding it. I thought when I read his exposition that it would have been a very capital comment upon the text if it had read, "Who *will not* have all men to be saved, nor come to a knowledge of the truth." Had such been the inspired language every remark of the learned doctor would have been exactly in keeping, but as it happens to say, "Who *will* have all men to be saved," his observations are more than a little out of place. My love of consistency with my own doctrinal views is not great enough to allow me knowingly to alter a single text of Scripture. I have great respect for orthodoxy, but my reverence for inspiration is far greater. I would sooner a hundred times over appear to be inconsistent with myself than be inconsistent with the word of God. I never thought it to be any very great crime to seem to be inconsistent with myself, for who am I that I should everlastingly be consistent? But I do think it a great crime to be so inconsistent with the word of God that I should want to lop away a bough or even a twig from so much as a single tree of the forest of Scripture. God forbid that I should cut or shape, even in the least degree, any divine expression. So runs the text, and so we must read it, "God our Saviour; who will have all men to be saved, and to come unto the knowledge of the truth."

Does not the text mean that it is the wish of God that men should be saved? The word "wish" gives as much force to the original as it really requires, and the passage should run thus—"whose wish it is that all men should be saved and come to a knowledge of the truth." As it is *my* wish that it should be so, as it is *your* wish that it might be so, so it is God's wish that all men should be saved; for, assuredly, he is not less benevolent than we are. Then comes the question, "But if he wishes it to be so, why does he not make it so?" Beloved friend, have you never heard that a fool may ask a question which a wise man cannot answer, and, if that be so, I am sure a wise person, like yourself, can ask me a great many questions which, fool as I am, I am yet not foolish enough to try to answer. Your question is only one form of the great debate of all the ages,—"If God be infinitely good and powerful, why does not his power carry out to the full all his beneficence?" It is God's wish that the oppressed should go free, yet there are many oppressed who are not free. It is God's wish that the sick should not suffer. Do you doubt it? Is it not your own wish? And yet the Lord does not work a miracle to heal every sick person. It is God's wish that his creatures should be happy. Do you deny that? He does not interpose by any miraculous agency to make us all happy, and yet it would be wicked to suppose that he does not wish the happiness of all the creatures that he has made. He has an infinite benevolence which, nevertheless, is not in all points worked out by his infinite omnipotence; and if anybody asked me why it is not, I cannot tell. I have never set up to be an explainer of all difficulties, and I have no desire to do so. It is the same old question as that of the negro who said, "Sare, you say the devil makes sin in the world." "Yes, the devil makes a deal of sin." "And you say that God hates sin." "Yes." "Then why does not he kill the devil and put an end to it?" Just so. Why does he not? Ah, my black friend, you will grow white before that question is answered. I cannot tell you why God permits moral evil, neither can the ablest philosopher on earth, nor the highest angel in heaven.

This is one of those things which we do not need to know. Have you never noticed that some people who are ill and are ordered to take pills are foolish enough to chew them? That is a very nauseous thing to do, though I have done it myself. The right way to take medicine of such a kind is to swallow it at once. In the same way there are some things in the Word of God which are undoubtedly true which must be swallowed at once by an effort of faith, and must not be chewed by perpetual questioning. You will soon have I know not what of doubt and difficulty and bitterness upon your soul if you must needs know the unknowable, and have reasons and explanations for the sublime and the mysterious. Let the difficult doctrines go down whole into your very soul, by a grand exercise of confidence in God.

I thank God for a thousand things I cannot understand. When I cannot get to know the reason why, I say to myself, "Why should I know the reason why? Who am I, and what am I, that I should demand explanations of my God?" I am a most unreasonable being when I am most reasonable, and when my judgment is most accurate I dare not trust it. I had rather trust my God. I am a poor silly child at my very best: my Father must know better than I. An old parable-maker tells us that he shut himself up in his study because he had to work out a difficult problem. His little child came knocking at the door, and he said "Go away, John: you cannot understand what father is doing; let father alone." Master Johnny for that very reason felt that he must get in and see what father was doing —a true symbol of our proud intellects; we must pry into forbidden things, and uncover that which is concealed. In a little time upon the sill, outside the window, stood Master Johnny, looking in through the window at his father; and if his father had not with the very tenderest care just taken him away from that very dangerous position, there would have been no Master Johnny left on the face of the earth to exercise his curiosity in dangerous elevations. Now, God sometimes shuts the door, and says, "My child, it is so: be content to believe." "But," we foolishly cry, "Lord, why is it so?" "It is so, my child," he says. "But why, Father, is it so?" "It is so, my child, believe me." Then we go speculating; climbing the ladders of reasoning, guessing, speculating, to reach the lofty windows of eternal truth. Once up there we do not know where we are, our heads reel, and we are in all kinds of uncertainty and spiritual peril. If we mind things too high for us we shall run great risks. I do not intend meddling with such lofty matters. There stands the text, and I believe that it is my Father's wish that "all men should be saved, and come to the knowledge of the truth." But I know, also, that he does not will it, so that he will save any one of them, unless they believe in his dear Son; for he has told us over and over that he will not. He will not save any man except he forsakes his sins, and turns to him with full purpose of heart: that I also know. And I know, also, that he has a people whom he will save, whom by his eternal love he has chosen, and whom by his eternal power he will deliver. I do not know how that squares with this; that is another of the things I do not know. If I go on telling you of all that I do not know, and of all that I do know, I will warrant you that the things that I do not know will be a hundred to one of the things that I do know. And so we will say no more about the matter, but just go on to the more practical part of the text. God's wish about man's salvation is this,—that men should be saved and come to the knowledge of the truth.

Men are saved, and the same men that are saved come to a knowledge of the truth. The two things happen together, and the two facts very much depend upon each other. God's way of saving men is not by leaving them in ignorance. It is by *a knowledge of the truth that men are saved;* this will make the main body of our discourse, and in closing we shall see how this truth *gives instruction to those who wish to be saved,* and also *to those who desire to save others.* May the Holy Spirit make these closing inferences to be practically useful.

Here is our proposition: IT IS BY A KNOWLEDGE OF THE TRUTH THAT MEN ARE SAVED.

Observe that stress is laid upon the article: it is *the* truth, and not every truth. Though it is a good thing to know the truth about anything, and we ought not to be satisfied to take up with a falsehood upon any point, yet it is not every truth that will save us. We are not saved by knowing any one theological truth we may choose to think of, for there are some theological truths which are comparatively of inferior value. They are not vital or essential, and a man may know them, and yet may not be saved. It is *the* truth which saves. Jesus Christ is *the* truth: the whole testimony of God about Christ is *the* truth. The work of the Holy Ghost in the heart is to work in us *the* truth. The knowledge of the truth is a large knowledge. It is not always so at the first: it may begin with but a little knowledge, but it is a large knowledge when it is further developed, and the soul is fully instructed in the whole range of the truth.

This knowledge of the grand facts which are here called the truth saves men, and we will notice its mode of operation. Very often it begins its work in a man by arousing him, and thus it *saves him from carelessness.* He did not know anything about the truth which God has revealed, and so he lived like a brute beast. If he had enough to eat and to drink he was satisfied. If he laid by a little money he was delighted. So long as the days passed pretty merrily, and he was free from aches and pains, he was satisfied. He heard about religion, but he thought it did not concern him. He supposed that there were some people who might be the better for thinking about it, but as far as he was concerned, he thought no more about God or godliness than the ox of the stall or the ostrich of the desert. Well, the truth came to him, and he received a knowledge of it. He knew only a part, and that a very dark and gloomy part of it, but it stirred him out of his carelessness, for he suddenly discovered that he was under the wrath of God. Perhaps he heard a sermon, or read a tract, or had a practical word addressed to him by some Christian friend, and he found out enough to know that "he that believeth not is condemned already, because he hath not believed on the Son of God." That startled him. "God is angry with the wicked every day:"—that amazed him. He had not thought of it, perhaps had not known it, but when he did know it, he could rest no longer. Then he came to a knowledge of this further truth, that after death there would be a judgment, that he would rise again, and that, being risen, he would have to stand before the judgment-seat of God to give an account of the things which he had done in the body. This came home very strikingly to him. Perhaps, also, such a text as this flamed forth before him,—"For every idle word that man shall speak he must give an account in the day of judgment." His mind began to foresee that last tremendous day, when on the clouds of heaven Christ will come and summon quick and dead, to answer at his judgment-seat for the whole of their lives. He did not know that before, but, knowing it, it startled and aroused him. I have known men, when first they have come to a knowledge of this truth, become unable to sleep. They have started up in the night. They have asked those who were with them to help them to pray. The next day they have been scarcely able to mind their business, for a dreadful sound has been in their ears. They feared lest they should stumble into the grave and into hell. Thus they were saved from carelessness. They could not go back to be the mere brute beasts they were before. Their eyes had been opened to futurity and eternity. Their spirits had been quickened—at least so much that they could not rest in that doltish, dull, dead carelessness in which they had formerly been found. They were shaken out of their deadly lethargy by a knowledge of the truth.

The truth is useful to a man in another way: *it saves him from prejudice.* Often when men are awakened to know something about the wrath of God they begin to plunge about to discover divers methods by which they may escape from that wrath. Consulting, first of all, with themselves, they think that, if they can reform—give up their grosser sins, and if they can join with religious people, they will make it all right. And there are some who go and listen to a kind of religious teacher, who says, "You must do good works. You must earn a good character. You must add to all this the ceremonies of our church. You must be particular and precise in receiving blessing only through the appointed channel of the apostolical succession." Of the aforesaid mystical succession this teacher has the effrontery to assure his dupe that he is a legitimate instrument; and that sacraments received at his hands are means of grace. Under such untruthful notions we have known people who were somewhat aroused sit down again in a false peace. They have done all that they judged right and attended to all that they were told. Suddenly, by God's grace, they come to a knowledge of another truth, and that is that by the deeds of the law there shall no flesh be justified in the sight of God. They discover that salvation is not by works of the law or by ceremonies, and that if any man be under the law he is also under the curse. Such a text as the following comes home, "Not of blood, nor of the will of the flesh, nor of the will of man, but of God"; and such another text as this, "Ye must be born again," and then this at the back of it—"that which is born of the flesh is flesh, and that which is born of the Spirit is spirit." When they also find out that there is necessary a righteousness better than their own —a perfect righteousness to justify them before God, and when they discover that they must be made new creatures in Christ Jesus, or else they must utterly perish, then they are saved from false confidences, saved from crying, "Peace, peace," when there is no peace. It is a grand thing when a knowledge of the truth stops us from trusting in a lie. I am addressing some who remember when they were saved in that way. What an opening of the eyes it was to you! You had a great prejudice against the gospel of grace and the plan of salvation by faith; but when the Lord took you in hand and made you see your beautiful righteousness to be a moth-eaten mass of rags, and when the gold that you had accumulated suddenly turned into so much brass, cankered, and good for nothing,—when you stood stripped naked before God, and the poor cobwebs of ceremonies suddenly dropped from off you, oh, then the Lord was working his salvation in your soul, and you were being saved from false confidences by a knowledge of the truth.

Moreover, it often happens that a knowledge of the truth stands a man in good stead for another purpose; *it saves him from despair*. Unable to be careless, and unable to find comfort in false confidences, some poor agitated minds are driven into a wide and stormy sea without rudder or compass, with nothing but wreck before them. "There is no hope for me," says the man. "I perceive I cannot save myself. I see that I am lost. I am dead in trespasses and sins, and cannot stir hand or foot. Surely now I may as well go on in sin, and even multiply my transgressions. The gate of mercy is shut against me; what is the use of fear where there is no room for hope?" At such a time, if the Lord leads the man to a knowledge of the truth, he perceives that though his sins be as scarlet they shall be as wool, and though they be red like crimson they shall be as white as snow. That precious doctrine of substitution comes in—that Christ stood in the stead of the sinner, that the transgression of his people was laid upon him, and that God, by thus avenging sin in the person of his dear Son, and honouring his law by the suffering of the Saviour, is now able to declare pardon to the penitent and grace to the believing. Now, when the soul comes to know that sin is put away by the atoning blood; when the heart discovers that it is not our life that saves us, but the life of God that comes to dwell in us; that we are not to be regenerated by our own actions, but are regenerated by the Holy Ghost who comes to us through the precious death of Jesus, then despair flies away, and the soul cries exultingly, "There is hope. There is hope. Christ died for sinners: why should I not have a part in that precious death? He came like a physician to heal the sick: why should he not heal me? Now I perceive that he does not want my goodness, but my badness; he does not need my righteousness, but my unrighteousness: for he came to save the ungodly and to redeem his people from their sins." I say, when the heart comes to a knowledge of this truth, then it is saved from despair; and this is no small part of the salvation of Jesus Christ.

A saving knowledge of the truth, to take another line of things, works in this way. A knowledge of the truth *shows a man his personal need of being saved.* O you that are not saved, and who dream you do not need to be, you only require to know the truth, and you will perceive that you must be saved or lost for ever.

A knowledge of the truth *reveals the atonement by which we are saved:* a knowledge of the truth *shows us what that faith is by which the atonement becomes available for us:* a knowledge of the truth teaches us that faith is the simple act of trusting, that it is not an action of which man may boast; it is not an action of the nature of a work, so as to be a fruit of the law; but faith is a self-denying grace which finds all its strength in him upon whom it lives, and lays all its honour upon him. Faith is not self in action but self forsaken, self abhorred, self put away that the soul may trust in Christ, and trust in Christ alone. There are persons now present who are puzzled about what faith is. We have tried to explain it a great many times to you, but we have explained it so that you did not understand it any the better; and yet the same explanation has savingly instructed others. May God the Holy Ghost open your understandings that you may practically know what faith is, and at once exercise it. I suppose that it is a very hard thing to understand because it is so plain. When a man wishes the way of salvation to be difficult he naturally kicks at it because it is easy; and, when his pride wants it to be hard to be understood, he is pretty sure to say that he does not understand it because it is so plain. Do not you know that the unlettered often receive Christ when philosophers refuse him, and that he who has not called many of the great, and many of the mighty, has chosen poor, foolish, and despised things? That is because poor foolish men, you know, are willing to believe a plain thing, but men wise in their own conceits desire to be, if they can, a little confounded and puzzled that they may please themselves with the idea that their own superior intellect has made a discovery; and, because the way of salvation is just so easy that almost an idiot boy may lay hold of it, therefore they pretend that they do not understand it. Some people cannot see a thing because it is too high up; but there are others who cannot see it because it is too low down. Now, it so happens that the way of salvation by faith is so simple that it seems beneath the dignity of exceedingly clever men. May God bring them to a knowledge of this truth: may they see that they cannot be saved except by giving up all idea of saving themselves; that they cannot be saved except they step right into Christ, for, until they get to the end of the creature, they will never get to the beginning of the Creator. Till they empty out their pockets of every mouldy crust, and have not a crumb left; they cannot come and take the rich mercy which is stored up in Christ Jesus for every empty, needy sinner. May the Lord be pleased to give you that knowledge of the truth !

When a man comes in very deed to a knowledge of the truth about faith in Christ, he trusts Christ, and he is there and then saved from the guilt of sin; and he begins to be saved altogether from sin. God cuts the root of the power of sin that very day; but yet it has such life within itself that at the scent of water it will bud again. Sin in our members struggles to live. It has as many lives as a cat: there is no killing it. Now, when we come to a knowledge of the truth, we begin to learn how sin is to be killed in us—how the same Christ that justifies, sanctifies, and works in us according to his working who worketh in us mightily, that we may be conformed to the image of Christ, and made meet to dwell with perfect saints above. Beloved, many of you that are saved from the guilt of sin, have a very hard struggle with the power of sin, and have much more conflict, perhaps, than you need to have, because you have not come to a knowledge of all the truth about indwelling sin. I therefore beg you to study much the word of God upon that point, and especially to see the adaptation of Christ to rule over your nature, and to conquer all your corrupt desires, and learn how by faith to bring each sin before him that, like Agag, it may be hewed in pieces before his eyes. You will never overcome sin except by the blood of the Lamb. There is no sanctification except by faith. The same instrument which destroys sin as to its guilt must slay sin as to its power. "They overcame by the blood of the Lamb," and so must you. Learn this truth well, so shall you find salvation wrought in you from day to day.

Now, I think I hear somebody say, "I think I know all about this." Yes, you may think you know it, and may not know anything at all about it. "Oh, but," says one, "I do know it. I learned the 'Assembly's Catechism' when I was a child. I have read the Bible ever since, and I am well acquainted with all the commonplaces of orthodoxy." That may be, dear friend, and yet you may not know the truth. I have heard of a man who knew how to swim, but, as he had never been in the water, I do not think much of his knowledge of swimming: in fact, he did not really know the art. I have heard of a botanist who understood all about flowers, but as he lived in London, and scarcely ever saw above one poor withered thing in a flowerpot, I do not think much of his botany. I have heard of a man who was a very great astronomer, but he had not a telescope, and I never thought much of his astronomy. So there are many persons who think they know and yet do not know because they have never had any personal acquaintance with the thing. A mere notional knowledge or a dry doctrinal knowledge is of no avail. We must know the truth in a very different way from that.

How are we to know it, then? Well, we are to know it, first, by *a believing knowledge*. You do not know a thing unless you believe it to be really so. If you doubt it, you do not know it. If you say, "I really am not sure it is true," then you cannot say that you know it. That which the Lord has revealed in holy Scripture you must devoutly believe to be true. In addition to this, your knowledge, if it becomes believing knowledge, must be *personal knowledge*—a persuasion that it is true in reference to yourself. It is true about your neighbour, about your brother, but you must believe it about *yourself*, or your knowledge is vain—for instance, you must know that *you* are lost—that *you* are in danger of eternal destruction from the presence of God—that for *you* there is no hope but in Christ—that for *you* there is hope if you rest in Christ—that resting in Christ *you* are saved. Yes, *you*. You must know that because you have trusted in Christ *you* are saved, and that now *you* are free from condemnation, and that now in *you* the new life has begun, which will fight against the old life of sin, until it overcome, and you, even you, are safely landed on the golden shore. There must be a personal appropriation of what you believe to be true. That is the kind of knowledge which saves the soul.

But this must be *a powerful knowledge*, by which I mean that it must operate in and upon your mind. A man is told that his house is on fire. I will suppose that standing here I held up a *telegram*, and said, "My friend, is your name so-and-so?" "Yes." "Well, your house is on fire." He knows the fact, does he not? Yes, but he sits quite still. Now, my impression is about that good brother, that he does not know, for he does not believe it. He cannot believe it, surely: he may believe that somebody's house is on fire, but not his own. If it is his house which is burning, and he knows it, what does he do? Why he gets up and goes off to see what he can do towards saving his goods. That is the kind of knowledge which saves the soul—when a man knows the truth about himself, and therefore his whole nature is moved and affected by the knowledge. Do I know that I am in danger of hell fire? And am I in my senses? Then I shall never rest till I have escaped from that danger. Do I know that there is salvation for me in Christ? Then I never shall be content until I have obtained that salvation by the faith to which that salvation is promised : that is to say, if I really am in my senses, and if my sin has not made me beside myself as sin does, for sin works a moral madness upon the mind of man, so that he puts bitter for sweet and sweet for bitter, and dances on the jaws of hell, and sits down and scoffs at Almighty mercy, despises the precious blood of Christ and will have none of it, although there and there only is his salvation to be found.

This knowledge when it comes really to save the soul is what we call *experimental knowledge*—knowledge acquired according to the exhortation of the psalmist, "Oh, taste and see that the Lord is good "—acquired by tasting. Now, at this present moment, I, speaking for myself, know that I am originally lost by nature. Do I believe it? Believe it? I am as sure of it as I am of my own existence. I know that I am lost by nature. It would not be possible for anybody to make me doubt that: I have felt it. How many weary days I spent under the pressure of that knowledge! Does a soldier know that there is such a thing as a cat when he has had a hundred lashes? It would take a deal of argument to make him believe there is not such a thing, or that backs do not smart when they feel the lash. Oh, how my soul smarted under the lash of conscience when I suffered under a sense of sin! Do I know that I could not save myself? Know it? Why, my poor, struggling heart laboured this way and that, even as in the very fire with bitter disappointment, for I laboured to climb to the stars on a treadwheel, and I was trying and trying and trying with all my might, but never rose an inch higher. I tried to fill a bottomless tub with leaking buckets, and worked on and toiled and slaved, but never accomplished even the beginning of my unhappy task. I know, for I have tried it, that salvation is not in man, or in all the feelings, and weepings, and prayings, and Bible readings, and church goings, and chapel goings which zeal could crowd together. Nothing whatsoever that man does can avail him towards his own salvation. This I know by sad trial of it, and failure in it.

But I do know that there is real salvation by believing in Christ. Know it? I have never preached to you concerning that subject what I do not know by experience. In a moment, when I believed in Christ I leaped from despair to fulness of delight. Since I have believed in Jesus I have found myself totally new—changed altogether from what I was; and I find now that, in proportion as I trust in Jesus, I love God and try to serve him; but if at any time I begin to trust in myself, I forget my God, and I become selfish and sinful. Just as I keep on being nothing and taking Christ to be everything, so am I led in the paths of righteousness. I am merely talking of myself, because a man cannot bear witness about other people so thoroughly as he can about himself. I am sure that all of you who have tried my Master can bear the same witness. You have been saved, and you have come to a knowledge of the truth experimentally; and every soul here that would be saved must in the same way believe the truth, appropriate the truth, act upon the truth, and experimentally know the truth, which is summed up in few words:—"Man lost: Christ his Saviour. Man nothing: God all in all. The heart depraved: the Spirit working the new life by faith." The Lord grant that these truths may come home to your hearts with power.

I am now going to draw two inferences which are to be practical. The first one is this: in regard TO YOU THAT ARE SEEKING SALVATION. Does not the text show you that it is very possible that the reason why you have not found salvation is because you do not know the truth? Hence, I do most earnestly entreat the many of you young people who cannot get rest to be very diligent searchers of your Bibles. The first thing and the main thing is to believe in the Lord Jesus Christ, but if you say, "I do not understand it," or "I cannot believe," or if there be any such doubt rising in your mind, then it may be because you have not gained complete knowledge of the truth. It is very possible that somebody will say to you, "Believe, believe, believe." I would say the same to you, but I should like you to act upon the common-sense principle of knowing what is to be believed and in whom you are to believe. I explained this to one who came to me a few evenings ago. She said that she could not believe. "Well," I said, "now suppose as you sit in that chair I say to you, 'Young friend, I cannot believe in you': you would say to me, 'I think you should.' Suppose I then replied, 'I wish I could.' What would you bid me do? Should I sit still and look at you till I said, 'I think I can believe in you'? That would be ridiculous. No, I should go and enquire, 'Who is this young person? What kind of character does she bear? What are her connections?' and when I knew all about you, then I have no doubt that I should say, 'I have made examination into this young woman's character, and I cannot help believing in her.'" Now, it is just so with Jesus Christ. If you say, "I cannot believe in him," read those four blessed testimonies of Matthew, Mark, Luke, and John, and especially linger much over those parts where they tell you of his death. Do you know that many, while they have been sitting, as it were, at the foot of the cross, viewing the Son of God dying for men, have cried out, "I cannot help believing. I cannot help believing. When I see my sin, it seems too great; but when I see my Saviour my iniquity vanishes away." I think I have put it to you sometimes like this: if you take a ride through London, from end to end, it will take you many days to get an idea of its vastness; for probably none of us know the size of London. After your long ride of inspection you will say, "I wonder how those people can all be fed. I cannot make it out. Where does all the bread come from, and all the butter, and all the cheese, and all the meat, and everything else? Why, these people will be starved. It is not possible that Lebanon with all its beasts, and the vast plains of Europe and America should ever supply food sufficient for all this multitude." That is your feeling. And then, to-morrow morning you get up, and you go to Covent Garden, you go to the great meat-markets, and to other sources of supply, and when you come home you say, "I feel quite different now, for now I cannot make out where all the people come from to eat all this provision: I never saw such store of food in all my life. Why, if there were two Londons, surely there is enough here to feed them." Just so—when you think about your sins and your wants you get saying, "How can I be saved?" Now, turn your thoughts the other way; think that Christ is the Son of God: think of what the merit must be of the incarnate God's bearing human guilt; and instead of saying, "My sin is too great," you will almost think the atoning sacrifice too great. Therefore I do urge you to try and know more of Christ; and I am only giving you the advice of Isaiah, "Incline your ear, and come unto me; hear, and your soul shall live." Know, hear, read, and believe more about these precious things, always with this wish—"I am not hearing for hearing's sake, and I am not wishing to know for knowing's sake, but I am wanting to hear and to know that I may be saved." I want you to be like the woman that lost her piece of silver. She did not light a candle and then say, "Bravo, I have lit a candle, this is enough." She did not take her broom and then sit down content, crying, "What a splendid broom." When she raised a dust she did not exclaim, "What a dust I am making! I am surely making progress now." Some poor sinners, when they have been seeking, get into a dust of soul-trouble, and think it to be a comfortable sign. No, I'll warrant you, the woman wanted her groat: she did not mind the broom, or the dust, or the candle; she looked for the silver. So it must be with you. Never content yourself with the reading, the hearing, or the feeling. It is Christ you want. It is the precious piece of money that you must find; and you must sweep until you find it. Why, there it is! There is Jesus! Take him! Take him! Believe him now, even now, and you are saved.

The last inference is for YOU WHO DESIRE TO SAVE SINNERS. You must, dear friends, bring *the truth* before them when you want to bring them to Jesus Christ. I believe that exciting meetings do good to some. Men are so dead and careless that almost anything is to be tolerated that wakes them up; but for real solid soul-work before God, telling men the truth is the main thing. What truth? It is gospel truth, truth about Christ that they want. Tell it in a loving, earnest, affectionate manner, for God wills that they should be saved, not in any other way, but in this way—by a knowledge of the truth. He wills that all men should be saved in this way—not by keeping them in ignorance, but by bringing the truth before them. That is God's way of saving them. Have your Bible handy when you are reasoning with a soul. Just say, "Let me call your attention to this passage." It has a wonderful power over a poor staggering soul to point to the Book itself. Say, "Did you notice this promise, my dear friend? And have you seen that passage?" Have the Scriptures handy. There is a dear brother of mine here whom God blesses to many souls, and I have seen him talking to some, and turning to the texts very handily. I wondered how he did it so quickly, till I looked in his Bible, and found that he had the choice texts printed on two leaves and inserted into the book, so that he could always open upon them. That is a capital plan, to get the cheering words ready to hand, the very ones that you know have comforted you and have comforted others. It sometimes happens that one single verse of God's word will make the light to break into a soul, when fifty days of reasoning would not do it. I notice that when souls are saved it is by our texts rather than by our sermons. God the Holy Ghost loves to use his own sword. It is God's word, not man's comment on God's word, that God usually blesses. Therefore, stick to the quotation of the Scripture itself, and rely upon *the truth*. If a man could be saved by a lie it would be a lying salvation. Truth alone can work results that are true. Therefore, keep on teaching *the truth*. God help you to proclaim the precious truth about the bleeding, dying, risen, exalted, coming Saviour; and God will bless it.

The Royal Prerogative

"He that is our God is the God of salvation; and unto God the Lord belong the issues from death. But God shall wound the head of his enemies, and the hairy scalp of such an one as goeth on still in his trespasses."—Psalm lxviii. 20, 21.

WHATEVER may be said of the Old Testament dispensation, however dimly it may have revealed certain truths, there was one matter about which it was clear as the sun. Under the Old Testament economy the Lord God of Israel is ever most conspicuous. God is in all, and over all; and from the pages of the prophets, as well as from the lips of the temple choirs, we hear loudly sounding forth the note, "The Lord shall reign for ever, even thy God, O Zion, unto all generations. Hallelujah!" By priest and prophet, saint and seer, the one testimony is borne, "The Lord reigneth." You cannot read the Book of Job without trembling in the majestic presence of the Almighty; nor can you turn to the Psalms without being filled with solemn awe as you see David, and Asaph, and Heman adoring the Lord, who made heaven and earth and the sea. Everywhere, from Abraham to Malachi, man is of small account, and God is all in all. Very little consideration is given to any fancied rights and claims of man, but wonder is expressed that the Creator should be mindful of him. We read no discourse upon the dignity of human nature, or upon the beauty of human character; but God alone is holy, and when he looks from heaven he sees none that doeth good, no, not one. Man is rolled in the dust from which he sprang, and to which he must return; all his pride is cut down, and his comeliness withered, and over all is seen one God, and none beside him.

It will be a great offence if, coming into the brighter light of the New Testament, we are less vivid in our conceptions of the glory of God. If God should be less clearly seen in the person of our Lord Jesus, than he was under the symbols of the law, it will be the fault of our blinded hearts. It will be ill for us to turn day into night, and like owls to see less because the light is increased. Let it not be so among us, but let it be in our churches as in Israel of old, of which it was said, "in Judah is God known; his name is great in Israel." "God, who at sundry times and in divers manners spake in time past unto the fathers by the

41

prophets, hath in these last days spoken unto us by his Son," and by him as the incarnate Word he has revealed himself with a sevenfold splendour, and therefore it should be our soul's great delight to perceive God in all things, to rejoice in his presence, and to magnify him in all things as King of kings and Lord of lords.

The Psalmist in this particular case ascribes to the Lord universal action and power over us, for he ascribes to him the mercies of life and the issues of death. He says, "Blessed be the Lord who daily loadeth us with benefits." The Lord heaps up his favours till their number loads the memory, and their value burdens the shoulders of gratitude. He gives us so many mercies that the mind is burdened in endeavouring to calculate their worth : we are overwhelmed with a sense of his goodness, and the consciousness that we cannot return any adequate thanks for such abundance of daily grace. Such is our God in life, and what will he be in death? Shall we be without him there? No, blessed be his name, "Unto God the Lord belong the issues from death." His kingdom includes the land of death-shade, and all the borders thereof. We shall not die without his permit, nor without his presence. Though temporal mercies will find their end when life ends, yet are there eternal mercies which throughout eternal life shall manifest the goodness of the Most High ; and meanwhile by rescues, recoveries, and escapes we shall be preserved from prematurely descending to the tomb. If any of you, dear friends, have been brought near to the gates of death, if you have been laid low by wearisome sickness, if your heart has sunk within you in a sort of mental death, you will in coming back to health and strength most heartily bless the Lord who finds for us a way of return from the suburbs of the sepulchre. He is not only the God of life but the God of death; he keeps us in life, and makes life happy ; he keeps us from death and from the fierce agencies which wait to drag us to the grave. There are issues out of the dark border-land of sickness, and peril, and despair, and the Lord leads us by his own right hand to cause us to escape. Doth he not say "I will bring again from Bashan, I will bring my people again from the depths of the sea"? We must, and we will praise him for this with a new song.

I gather from our text that death is in the hand of God, that escapes from death are manifestations of his divine power, and that he is to be praised for them.

The outline of this morning's discourse, as indicated by the text, is just this : first, *the sovereign prerogative of God,* "To God the Lord belong the issues from death": secondly, *the character of the sovereign* with whom this prerogative is lodged, "He that is our God is the God of salvation": and then, thirdly, *the solemn warning which this great sovereign gives* in reference to the exercise of his prerogative; weighty are the words, may the Holy Spirit cause us to feel their power—"God shall wound the head of his enemies, and the hairy scalp of such an one as goeth on still in his trespasses."

I. First, then, with deep reverence let us speak upon THE SOVEREIGN PREROGATIVE OF GOD—"Unto God the Lord belong the issues from death." Kings have been accustomed to keep the power of life and death in their own hands. The great King of kings, the sovereign Ruler and absolute Lord of all worlds reserves this to himself.—that he shall permit men to die, or shall give them an issue from death at his own good will and pleasure. He can alike create and destroy. He sendeth forth his Spirit and they are created, and at his own pleasure he saith, " Return, ye children of men," and lo! they fall before him like autumn's faded leaves.

The prerogative of life or death belongs to God in a wide range of senses. First of all as to natural life, we are all dependent upon his good pleasure. We shall not die until the time which he appoints; for our death-time, like all our time, is in his hands. Our skirts may brush against the portals of the sepulchre, and yet we shall pass the iron gate unharmed if the Lord be our guard. The wolves of disease will hunt us in vain until God shall permit them to overtake us. The most desperate enemies may waylay us, but no bullet shall find its billet in any heart unless the Lord allows it. Our life does not even depend upon the care of angels, nor can our death be compassed by the malice of devils. We are immortal till our work is done, immortal till the immortal King shall call us home to the land where we shall be immortal in a still higher sense. When we are most sick, and most ready to faint into the grave, we need not despair of recovery, since the issues from death are in Almighty hands. "The Lord killeth and maketh alive: he bringeth down to the grave and bringeth up." When we have passed beyond the skill of the physician we have not passed beyond the succour of our God, to whom belong the issues from death.

Spiritually, too, this prerogative is with God. We are by nature under the condemnation of the law on account of our sins, and we are like criminals tried, convicted, sentenced, and left for death. It is for God, as the great Judge, to see the sentence executed, or to issue a free pardon, according as he pleases; and he will have us know that it is upon his supreme pleasure that this matter depends. Over the head of a universe of sinners I hear this sentence thundering, " I will have mercy on whom I will have mercy, and I will have compassion on whom I will have compassion." Shut up for death, as men are by reason of their sins, it rests with God to pardon whom he may reserve; none have any claim to his favour, and it must be exercised upon mere prerogative, because he is the Lord God, merciful and gracious, and delighteth to pass by transgression and sin.

So, too, doth the Lord deliver his own believing people from those " deaths oft " which make up their experience. Though we are in Christ Jesus delivered from death as a penalty, yet we often feel an inward death, caused by the old nature, which exercises a deadening influence within us. We feel the sentence of death in ourselves that we may not trust in ourselves, but in Jesus, in whom our life is hid. It may be that for a season our joys are damped, our spiritual vigour is drained away, and we hardly know whether we have any spiritual life left within us. We become like the trees in winter, whose substance is in them but the sap ceases to flow, and there is neither fruit nor leaf to betray the secret life within. We scarcely feel a spiritual emotion in these sad times, and dare not write ourselves among the living in Zion. At such times God the Lord can give us back the fulness of life, he can restore our soul from the pit of corruption and cause us not only to have life but to have it more abundantly. The issues from death are with the quickening

Spirit, and when our soul cleaveth to the dust he can revive us again till we rejoice with joy unspeakable.

As the climax of all, when we shall come actually to die, and these bodies of ours shall descend into the remorseless grave, as probably they will, in the hands of our Redeeming Lord are the issues from death. The archangel is even now waiting for the signal: one blast of his trumpet shall suffice to gather the chosen from all lands, from the east and from the west, from the south and from the north. Then death itself shall die away, and the righteous shall arise

> " From beds of dust and silent clay
> To realms of everlasting day."

" I am the resurrection and the life," saith Christ, and he is both of these to all his people. Is he not life, for he saith, " Whosoever liveth and believeth in me shall never die"? Is he not resurrection, for he saith, " He that believeth in me, though he were dead, yet shall he live"? That bright illustrious day in which the saints shall rise with their Lord will show how unto God the Lord belong the issues from death.

Our translation is a very happy one, because it bears so many renderings, and includes not only escape from death, deliverance from condemnation, revival from spiritual death, and uplifting from deadly mental depression, but recovery from death's direct havoc, by our being raised again from the tomb. In all these respects the Lord Jesus hath the key of death; he openeth and no man shutteth, he shutteth and no man openeth.

Concerning this prerogative we may say, first, that to God belongs *the right to exercise it.* This right springs, first, from his being our Creator. He saith " all souls are mine." He has an absolute right to do with us as he pleases, seeing he hath made us, and not we ourselves. Men forget what they are, and boast great things; but truly they are but as clay on the potter's wheel, and he can fashion them or can break them as he pleases. They think not so, but he knoweth their thoughts, that they are vain. Oh the dignity of man! What a theme for a sarcastic discourse! As the frog in the fable swelled itself till it burst asunder, so doth man in his pride and envy against his Maker, who nevertheless sitteth upon the circle of the heavens, and reckoneth men as though they were grasshoppers, and regardeth whole nations of them as the small dust of the balance. The Lord's prerogative of creation is manifestly widened morally by our forfeiture of any consideration which might have arisen out of obedience and rectitude if we had possessed them. Our fault has involved forfeiture of the creature's claims, whatever they may have been. We are all attainted of high treason, and we have each one been guilty of personal rebellion, and therefore we have not the rights of citizens, but lie under sentence of condemnation. What saith the infallible voice of God? " Cursed is every one that continueth not in all things that are written in the book of the law to do them." We have come under this curse; justice has pronounced us guilty, and by nature we abide under condemnation. If then the Lord shall be pleased to deliver us from death it rests with him to do so, but we have no right to any such deliverance, nor can we urge any argument which would avail in the courts of justice for reversal of sentence or stay of execution. Before the bar of justice our case must go hard if we set up up any plea of right. We shall be driven away with the disdain of the impartial Judge if we urge our suit upon that line. Our wisest course is to appeal to his mercy and to his sovereign grace, for there alone is our hope. Understand me clearly: if the Lord shall suffer us all to perish we shall only receive our deserts, and we have not one of us a shade of claim upon his mercy: we are therefore absolutely in his hands, and to him belong the issues from death.

This right of God to save is further made manifest by the redemption of his people. It might have been said that God had no right to save if by saving he would abridge his justice; but now that he hath laid help upon one that is mighty, and his only-begotten Son has become a victim in our place, to magnify the law and make it honourable, the Lord God hath an unquestionable right to deliver from death his own redeemed, for whom the Substitute has died. Our God saves his people in consistency with justice: no one can question his doing right even when he justifies the ungodly. His right and power over the issues from death are in the case of his own blood-bought ones clear as the sun at noon-day, and who shall dispute with him?

Our text, however, puts the prerogative upon the one sole ground of lordship, and we prefer to come back to that. "Unto God *the Lord* belong the issues from death." It is a doctrine which is very unpalatable in these days, but one nevertheless which is to be held and taught, that God is an absolute sovereign, and doeth as he wills. The words of Paul may not be suffered to sleep,—"Nay, but O man, who art thou that repliest against God? Shall the thing formed say to him that formed it, why hast thou made me thus?" The Lord cannot do amiss, his perfect nature is a law unto itself. In his case *Rex* is *Lex*, the King is the law. He is the source and fountain of all right, truth, rule, and order. Being absolutely perfect within himself, and comprehending all things, it is not possible for him to do otherwise than right. He is goodness, truth, and righteousness itself, and therefore the prerogatives of his throne are not bounded, and to the Lord of heaven and earth belong the issues from death.

Enough with regard to that matter of right. I go on to notice that *the Lord has the power of this prerogative.* With him is the ability to deliver men from natural death. Jehovah Rophi is a physician who is never baffled. Medicines may fail, but not the great Maker of all plants and herbs and useful drugs. Study and experience may be at a nonplus, but he who fashioned the human frame knows its most intricate parts, and can soon correct its disorders. God can restore when a hundred diseases are upon us all at once. Take courage, thou fainting one, and look up. Certainly, as to the soul, there is no case of man so far gone that God cannot find an issue out of its death. He can cast out seven devils, and a legion of diabolical sins. To God the Lord belong the issues from death, however foul the sin, and however forlorn the condition caused by transgression. He who raised Lazarus from the grave after four days can raise the most corrupt from the grave of their iniquities. O that awakened sinners would believe this!

I remember reading of an aged minister who had for some years fallen into deep despondency. He gave up his pulpit, and kept himself very much alone, always writing bitter things against himself. At last, when he was on a sick bed, a servant of God was sent to him, who dealt wisely with him. This good man said to the despairing one, " Brother, do you believe that passage, 'He is able also to save them to the uttermost that come unto God by him'?" " I believe it," said he, " with all my heart, but I am convinced—" Here the other stopped him, " I do not ask what your convincements may be, nor what your feelings may be, but I come to say to you, the man who trusts that promise lives." This plain declaration of the gospel was made by the divine Comforter the means of supreme consolation to the despairing one; may it be equally useful to all those who hear it. He who can hang his soul's hope upon the infinite ability of Christ to save is a saved man. He that believeth on him hath everlasting life. What a blessing this is ! The devil may tell me that I never can issue out of deserved death, and that I am shut up for ever under the just results of my trespasses ; my own conscience knowing my undeservingness may also condemn me a thousand times over; but unto God the Lord belong the issues from death, and he can and will pluck me from between the jaws of death since I believe in him. He is able to bring up those whom he ordains to save even from the utmost depths of despair. The absolute right of God is supported by almighty power, and thus his prerogative is made a matter of fact.

Nor is this all, *the Lord has actually exercised this prerogative* in abundant cases. As to those issues from death which are seen in restoration from sickness, I need not remind you that these are plentiful enough. At times these have come in a miraculous form, as when Hezekiah had his life lengthened in answer to prayer, and when many others were healed by the Saviour and his apostles. Life has been preserved in a lion's den, and in the belly of a fish, in a fiery furnace, and in the heart of the sea. Death has no arrow in his quiver which can hurt the man whom God ordains to live. Out of imminent peril the Lord still delivers in the ordinary course of providence, and there are persons present this morning who are proofs of his interposing power. He has raised some of us from prostration of body and depression of spirit, he has rescued others from shipwreck and fire in very singular ways, and here we are, living to praise God, as we do this day.

God has exercised this prerogative spiritually. In what a myriad of cases has he delivered souls from death ! Ask yon white-robed hosts in heaven, " Has not God displayed in you his sovereign power to save?" Ask many here below, who have tasted that he is gracious, and they will tell, " He saved me." According to his mercy he has issued a free pardon, signed by his royal hand, saying, " Deliver him from going down into the pit, for I have found a ransom." Why his sovereignty has interposed to rescue us from death we cannot tell. We often ask, " Why was I made to hear his voice? How was it that I was made to live?" But we are silent with grateful wonder, and invent no answer. Divine will, backed by divine power, worked out the sovereign purpose of love, and here we are, saved from so great a death by love invincible.

Yes, indeed, to God the Lord belong the issues from death. Come, then, brethren and sisters, *let him have all the glory of it.* If you are alive after a long sickness, bless the Lord, who forgiveth all our iniquities, who healeth all our diseases. If you are saved from condemnation this morning, and know it, bless the Lord, who accepts us in the beloved. If you feel at this moment that the death of sin has no dominion over you, for the life of grace reigns within, then bless the Lord who has quickened you into newness of life. Glorify his name this day, who in love to your soul has delivered you from the pit of corruption, and cast all your sins behind his back. Once more, if you have a glorious hope of a blessed resurrection, and feel that you can smile on death because God smiles on you, then bless the Lord who will raise you up at the last day. Your Redeemer liveth, and you shall live because he lives, therefore clap your hands with holy glee. Bless the all-glorious name of him to whom belong the issues from death.

II. Thus have I set forth the prerogative; and now, secondly, follow me with your thoughts while I show THE CHARACTER OF THE SOVEREIGN in whom that prerogative is vested. We cannot upon this earth exhibit much love to human princes who claim absolute dominion. Imperialism is not to our mind. Among the worst curses that have ever fallen upon mankind have been absolute monarchs: nowadays men shake them off as Paul shook off the viper into the fire. The Lord grant we may see the last of all despotic dynasties, that the nations may be free. We cannot endure a tyrant, and yet if we could have absolutely perfect despots it might be the best possible form of government. Assuredly, the great and eternal God, who is King of kings and Lord of lords, is absolutely perfect; and we may be well content to leave all prerogatives and vest all powers in his hands. He has never trampled on the rights of the meanest, nor forgotten the weakest. His foot doth not needlessly crush a worm, nor doth he beat down a fly in wantonness. He has never done a wrong, nor wrought an injustice. We oppress each other, but the Judge of all oppresses none. The Lord is holy in all his ways, and his mercy endureth for ever; and the amplest prerogatives are safely lodged in such hands.

Our text yet further tells us who it is in whose hands the issues of life and death are left: "He that is our God is the God of salvation." Sinner, your salvation rests with God, but do not therefore be discouraged, for that God with whom the matter rests is the God of salvation, or of "salvations," for so the Hebrew hath it. What mean we by this?

The Scripture signifieth, first, that *salvation is the most glorious of all God's designs.* Since this world was made, the working out of salvation has run through history like a silver thread. The Lord made the world, and lit up moon and stars, and set heaven, earth, and sea in order, with his eye upon salvation in the whole arrangement. He has ruled all things by his supreme government with the same end. The great wheels of his providence have been revolving these six thousand years before the eyes of men, and among them, and at their back, a hand has been ever passing to conduct every movement to the ultimate issue, which is the salvation of the covenanted ones. This is the object which is dearest to Jehovah's heart. He loves best to save. God was pleased with creation, but not as he is with redemption. When he made the heavens and the earth it was every-day work to him, and he merely spake and said, "It is good"; but when he gave his Son to die to redeem his people, and his elect were being saved, he did not speak with the prosaic brevity of creation, but he sang. Is it not written, "He shall rest in his love, he shall rejoice over thee with singing"? Redemption is a matter which Jehovah sings about. Are you able to imagine what it must be for God to sing? For Father, Son, and Holy Ghost to burst forth into a joyous hymn over the work of salvation! This is because salvation is dearest to God's heart, and in it his whole nature is most intensely engaged. Judgment is his strange work, but he delighteth in mercy. He has put forth many attributes in the accomplishment of other works, but in this he has laid out all his being. He is seen in this as mighty to save. Herein he hath bared his arm. For this he has taken his Son out of his bosom. For this he has caused his Only-begotten to be bruised and put to grief. Salvation is the eternal purpose of the inmost heart of God, and by it his highest glory is revealed. This, then, is the God to whom belong the issues from death : the God whose grandest design is salvation. Sing unto his name and exult that the Lord reigneth, even the Lord who is my strength and my song, who also hath become my salvation.

Ask ye yet again what this meaneth—" He that is our God is the God of salvation," and we remind you that *the most delightful works which the Lord has performed have been works of salvation.* To save our first parents at Eden's gate, and give them a promise of victory over the serpent, was joy to God. To house Noah in the ark was also his pleasure. The drowning of a guilty world was needful, but the saving of Noah was pleasant to the Lord our God. He destroyed the earth with his left hand, but with his right hand he shut in the only righteous ones he found. To save his people is ever his joy : he goes about it eagerly. He rode upon a cherub and did fly, yea, he did fly upon the wings of the wind when he came to deliver his chosen. What noise he makes about his saving work at the Red Sea! The whole Scripture is full of allusions to the great salvation out of Egyptian bondage, and even in heaven they sing the song of Moses, the servant of God, and the song of the Lamb. The Old Testament seems to ring with the note, "Sing unto the Lord for he hath triumphed gloriously, the horse and his rider hath he thrown into the sea." The Lord did greatly rejoice to make a way through the wilderness, and a path through the deeps for his own people, that he might work salvation for them in the midst of the earth. Afterwards in the Old Testament how well they keep the records of salvations! They tell us of the kings that oppressed the people, but how lovingly they linger over the way in which God redeemed Israel from her adversaries. What a note of joy there is about Goliath slain, and the son of Jesse bearing his gory head, and Israel delivered from Philistia's vaunts! Well did they say, "He that is our God is the God of salvation." He takes delight in deeds of grace : these are his enjoyments. These are his recreations. He comes out in his royal robes and puts on his crown jewels when he rises to save his people, and therefore his servants cry aloud, "O bless our God, ye people, and make the voice of his praise to be heard ; which holdeth our soul in life, and suffereth not our feet to be moved." This then is the God in whom is vested all sovereignty over the issues from death. He takes pleasure, not in the destruction, but in the salvation of the sons of men. Where could the prerogative be better laid up?

"He that is our God is the God of salvation," also means that at this present time the God who is preached to us is the God of salvation. *We live at this moment under the dispensation of mercy.* The sword is sheathed, the scales of justice are put by. Those scales are not destroyed, and that sword is not broken, nor even blunted, but for a while it slumbereth in its scabbard. To-day over all our heads is held out the silver sceptre of eternal love. The angelic carol, first heard by shepherds at Bethlehem, lingers still in the upper air, if you have ears to hear it,—" Glory to God in the highest, and on earth peace, good will toward men." The mediatorial reign of Christ is that of multiplied salvations. "Come unto me, all ye that labour and are heavy laden, and I will give you rest" is the saving proclamation of the reigning God. The God of the Christian age is the God of salvation. He is set forth before us as coming to seek and to save the lost. He dwells among us by his abiding Spirit, not as a Judge punishing criminals, but as a Father receiving his wandering children to his bosom, and rejoicing over them as once dead but now alive again. God in Christ Jesus, our God and Saviour Jesus Christ, is he, who quickeneth whom he will, and is ordained to give eternal life to as many as the Father hath given him. Where else could all power be more safely laid up ?

Once more : " He that is our God is the God of salvation " means this, that to his covenanted ones, *to those who can call him " our God" he is specially and emphatically the God of salvation.* There is no destruction for those who call him " our God," for " there is therefore now no condemnation to them that are in Christ Jesus." Jesus came not to condemn the world, but that the world through him might be saved. " This God is our God for ever and ever, he will be"—our destroyer?—no, " he will be our guide even unto death." This God is our sun and shield, and he will give grace and glory. Now, mark well this fact: we who believingly call the Lord our God this morning will tell you that we are saved entirely through the sovereign grace of God, and not through any natural betterness of our own, nor through anything that we have done to deserve his favour. It was because he looked upon us with pity and kindly regard when we were dead in sin that therefore we live. When we were lying in our blood, and in our filthiness, he passed by in the time of love, and he said to us, " Live." If he had passed by, and left us to die, he would have been infinitely just in so doing, but his heart was otherwise inclined. He looked on us and said " Live," and we lived, and we bless his name that we are living still, and praising his eternal and infinite mercy. He who saith " I kill and I make alive, I wound and I heal," is he who has quickened us, though we were dead in trespasses and sins. Surely, he who has exercised his prerogative so kindly towards us may be trusted to exercise it towards all who come to him according to his gracious invitation. If there be any man who saith, " I rejoice in the election of God, because, although he hath saved me, he hath left others to perish," I desire to have no sympathy with his spirit. My joy is of a far different kind, for I argue that he who saved such an unworthy one as I am will cast out none that come to him by faith. His election is not narrow, for it comprehends a number that no man can number, yea, all that will believe in Jesus. He waiteth to be gracious, and him that cometh to him he will in no wise cast out. The wedding feast needs countless guests, and every seat must be filled. We wish that all the human race would come and accept the provisions of infinite love, and we are anxious to go into the highways and hedges and compel them to come in. We rejoice to know that if any man be shut out from Christ and hope he shuts himself out, though at the same time we feel that if any man be shut in he did not shut himself in, but undeserved grace wrought out his salvation. Justice rules in condemnation, but grace reigns in salvation. In salvation we must ascribe all to grace, absolutely and unreservedly. There must be no stammering over this truth. Some begin to say grace, but they do not out with the word : they stutter it into "free-will." This will never do. This is not according to the teaching of Holy Scripture, nor is it in accordance with fact. If there is any man here who thinks that he has been saved as the result of his own will, apart from the powerful grace of God, let him throw his cap up, and magnify himself for ever. "Glory be to my own good disposition !" But as for me, I will fall at the foot of the throne of God, and say, "Grace reigns through righteousness unto eternal life by Jesus Christ. Hadst thou, O God, left me to my own free will, I had continued still to despise thy love, and to reject thy mercy." Surely, all the people of God agree that this is the fact in their own case, however they may differ theoretically from the general statement.

Yes, the prerogative of life and death is in good hands, it is in the hands of him who is the God of our salvation, and I beseech every one here present who is not saved to be encouraged to bow before the throne of the great King, and sue for mercy of him who is so ready to save. Go home and try to merit salvation, and you will waste your efforts. Go about to fit yourself for mercy, and to fashion some good that may attract the regard of God, and you will befool yourselves, and insult the majesty of heaven : but come just as you are, all guilty, empty, meritless, and fall before the great King, whom you have so often provoked, and beseech him of his infinite mercy to blot out your transgressions, to change your natures, and to make you his own, and see if he will cast you away. Is it not written, "There is forgiveness with thee, that thou mayest be feared"? And again, "Him that cometh to me I will in no wise cast out." His throne is a throne of grace. Mercy is built up for ever before him. He is the Lord God, merciful and gracious, slow to anger, and plenteous in mercy. Did ever a penitent sue for pardon at his sovereign feet to be rejected? Never; nor shall such a case happen while the earth remaineth. If you try to purchase his favour you shall be refused; if you claim it as a right you shall be rejected; but if you will come and accept salvation of the divine charity, and receive it through the atonement of Christ Jesus, the Lord will find for you an escape from death. Hear the witness of Jeremiah, and be encouraged to cast yourself before the Lord :—"I called upon thy name, O Lord, out of the low dungeon. Thou hast heard my voice : hide not thine ear at my breathing, at my cry. Thou drewest near in the day that I called upon thee : thou saidst, fear not. O Lord, thou hast pleaded the causes of my soul; thou hast redeemed my life."

III. Our last duty is to hear THE SOLEMN WARNING OF OUR SOVEREIGN LORD. A new god has been lately set up among men, the god of modern Christianity, the god of modern thought, a god made of honey or sugar of lead. He is all leniency, gentleness, mildness, and indifference in the matter of sin. Justice is not in him, and as for the punishment of sin, he knows it not. The Old Testament, as you are, no doubt, made aware by the wise men of this world, takes a very harsh view of God, and therefore modern wisdom sets it on one side. Forsooth, one half the word of God is out of date, and turned to waste paper. Although our Lord Jesus did not come "to destroy the law or the prophets," but to fulfil them, yet the advanced thinkers of these enlightened times tell us that the idea of God in the Old Testament is a false one. We are to believe in a new god, who does not care whether we do right or wrong, for by his arrangement all will come to the same end in the long run. There may be a little twisting about for awhile for some who are rather incorrigible, but it will all come right at last. Live as you like, go and swear and drink, go and oppress the nations, and make bloody wars, and act as you will; by jingo you will be all right at last. This is roughly the modern creed which poisons all our literature. But let me say, by Jehovah this shall not be as men dream. Jehovah, the Judge of all the earth, must do right. The God of Abraham, and of Isaac, and of Jacob is the God of our Lord and Saviour Jesus Christ: the God of the whole earth shall he be called. He hath not changed one whit in the stern integrity of his nature, and he will by no means spare the guilty. Read, then, the last verse of our text, and believe that it is as true to-day as when it was first written, and that if Jesus himself were here, the meek and lowly one would say it in tones of tearful solemnity, but he would utter it none the less. "God shall wound the head of his enemies, and the hairy scalp of such an one as goeth on still in his trespasses."

It is clear from these words that God is not indifferent to human character. Our God knows his enemies, he does not mistake them for friends, nor treat them as such. He regards iniquity as a trespass, and therefore he has not broken down the bounds of law, nor the hedges of right: there are trespasses still, and God perceives them, and notes them down, and such as go on in their trespasses are trying his long-suffering and provoking his justice. God sleeps not, neither does he wink at human sin, but calls upon all men everywhere to repent.

And it is clear too that God has the power to smite those who rebel against him. Dream not of natural laws which will screen the wicked— "He shall wound the head of his enemies." They may lift up those heads as high as they please, but they cannot be beyond the reach of his hand. He will not merely bruise their heels, or wound them on the back with blows which may be healed, but at their heads he will aim fatal blows, and lay them in the dust. He can do it, and he will. They may be very strong, and their scalp covered with hair may indicate unabated strength, but they cannot resist omnipotence. There may be no sign as yet of the baldness which comes of weakness, or of the scantiness of hair which is a token of old age, but vain are they who boast their vigour, for in their prime he can cause them to wither as the grass of the field. The proud may vaunt themselves of their beauty: their hairy scalp, like that of Absalom, may be their boast, but as the Lord made the hair of Absalom to be the instrument of his doom, so can he make the glory of man to be his ruin. Pride goeth before destruction, and a haughty spirit before a fall. No man is out of the reach of God, and no nation either. The great ones stand on high upon their lofty places, and they talk about the "vulgar crowd," and despise the godly of the land. As for foreign races, how lightly are they esteemed, though one God has made them all. Populations and nations, what are they? Mere food for powder when a proud nation is set upon its own aggrandizement. Overturn their kingdoms, slaughter their patriotic defenders, redden the earth with blood, burn their houses, starve their women and children. Doth God know, and is there judgment in the Most High? We are a great people, and have the men, the ships, and the money. Who shall call us to account? Yet let the still small voice be heard. Thus said the Lord to a great nation of old, "Thou hast trusted in thy wickedness: thou hast said, None seeth me. Thou hast said in thine heart, I am, and none else beside me. Therefore shall evil come upon thee; thou shalt not know from whence it riseth: and mischief shall fall upon thee; thou shalt not be able to put it off: and desolation shall come upon thee suddenly, which thou shalt not know." From such chastisements good Lord deliver us.

When the Lord does put his hand to the work of vengeance his smiting will be terrible, even an utter overthrow, for it will be a smiting upon the head. If he doth not smite his enemies until the hour of death, what a blow will they then receive! They boasted of their self-righteousness, or of their greatness; but, oh, what terror will seize them when at the last moment, while they dream of heaven they are smitten down into the unfathomable deep, where woe shall be the everlasting reward of their daring rebellion against their King! Warriors of old times would when they went to battle often shave off all their hair, except those locks which are on the hinder part of the scalp; yet when they turned to flee it frequently happened they were grasped by their pursuers by their flowing hair. God does not often take the wicked by the forelock, for he has great patience, and bears with them. In special cases, as when young men through dissipated habits hasten on their doom, he takes them in front; but as a rule he waits in mercy, and yet he suffers them not to go unpunished, for at the last he seizes their hairy scalp. If for fourscore years infinite patience should permit a man to continue in his rebellion, yet if he goeth on in his trespasses at the very last God shall thrust his hand into his hairy scalp and grasp him to his destruction.

Turn ye, then, ye that know not God, turn ye at his rebuke this morning, for the rebuke is meant in love; and if I have used hard words it is because my heart is honestly anxious that you would repent and escape to him who hath in his power the issues from death. I am not like yon flatterers who tell you that there is a little hell and a little God, from which you naturally infer that you may live as you like. Both you and they will perish everlastingly if you believe them. There is a dreadful hell, for there is a righteous God. Turn ye to him, I entreat you, while yet in Christ Jesus he sets mercy before you. He is the God of salvation, and entreats you to come and accept of his great grace in Christ Jesus.

The Lord bless this word according to his own mind, and unto him be praise for ever and ever. Amen.

The Plain Man's Pathway to Peace

"And when Jesus departed thence, two blind men followed him, crying, and saying, Thou son of David, have mercy on us. And when he was come into the house, the blind men came to him: and Jesus saith unto them, Believe ye that I am able to do this? They said unto him, Yea, Lord. Then touched he their eyes, saying, According to your faith be it unto you. And their eyes were opened; and Jesus straitly charged them, saying, See that no man know it."—Matthew ix. 27—30.

I AM not about to expound this incident, nor to draw illustrations from it, but only to direct your attention to one single point in it, and that is, its extreme simplicity. There are other cases of blind men, and we have various incidents connected with them, such as in one instance the making of clay, and the sending of the patient to wash at the pool of Siloam, and so forth. But here the cure is extremely simple: the men are blind, they cry to Jesus, they come near, they confess their faith, and they receive their sight straightway. In many other cases of miracles that were wrought by Christ there were circumstances of difficulty; in one case a man is let down through the tiling, being borne of four; in a second case a woman comes behind him in the press, and touches the hem of his garment with great effort; we read of another who had been dead four days already, and there seemed to be a clear impossibility in the way of his ever coming forth from the tomb; but everything is plain sailing here. Here are blind men, conscious of their blindness, confident that Christ can give them sight, they cry to him, they come to him, they believe that he is able to open their eyes and they receive their sight at once.

You see there was, in their case, these simple elements,—a sense of blindness, a desire for sight; then prayer, then coming to Christ, then an open avowal of faith, and then the cure. The whole matter lies in a nutshell. There are no details, no points of care and nicety which might suggest anxiety: the whole business is simplicity itself, and upon that one point I want to dwell at this time.

There are cases of conversion which are just as simple as this case of the opening of the eyes of the blind; and we are not to doubt the reality of the work of grace in them because of the remarkable absence of singular incidents and striking details. We are not to suppose that a conversion is a less genuine work of the Holy Ghost because it is extremely simple. May the Holy Spirit bless our meditation.

I. To make our discourse useful to many I will begin by remarking, in the first place, that it is an undoubted fact that MANY PERSONS ARE MUCH TROUBLED IN COMING TO CHRIST.

It is a fact which must be admitted, that all do not come quite so readily as these blind men came. There are instances on record in biographies—there are many known to us, and perhaps our own cases are among them—in which coming to Christ was a matter of struggle, of effort, of disappointment, of long waiting, and at last of a kind of desperation by which we were forced to come. You must have read Mr. John Bunyan's description of how the pilgrims came to the wicket gate. They were pointed, you remember, by Evangelist to a light and to a gate, and they went that way according to his bidding. I have told you sometimes the story of a young man in Edinburgh who was very anxious to speak to others about their souls; so he addressed himself one morning to an old Musselburgh fishwife, and he began by saying to her, "Here you are with your burden." "Ay," said she. He asked her, "Did you ever feel a spiritual burden?" "Yes," she said, resting a bit, "I felt the spiritual burden years ago, before you were born, and I got rid of it, too; but I did not go the same way to work that Bunyan's pilgrim did." Our young friend was greatly surprised to hear her say that, and thought she must be under grievous error, and therefore begged her to explain. "No," said she, "when I was under concern of soul, I heard a true gospel minister, who bade me look to the cross of Christ, and there I lost my load of sin. I did not hear one of those milk-and-water preachers like Bunyan's Evangelist." "How," said our young friend, "do you make that out?" "Why, that Evangelist, when he met the man with the burden on his back, said to him, 'Do you see that wicket gate?' 'No,' said he, 'I don't.' 'Do you see that light?' 'I think I do.' Why, man," said she, "he should not have spoken about wicket gates or lights, but he should have said, 'Do you see Jesus Christ hanging on the cross? Look to him, and your burden will fall off your shoulder.' He sent that man round the wrong way when he sent him to the wicket gate, and much good he got by it, for he was likely to have been choked in the slough of despond before long. I tell you, I looked at once to the cross, and away went my burden." "What," said this young man, "did you never go through the slough of despond?" "Ah," said she, "many a time, more than I care to tell. But at the first I heard the preacher say, 'Look to Christ,' and I looked to him. I have been through the slough of despond since that; but let me tell you, sir, it is much easier to go through that slough with your burden off than it is with your burden on." And so it is. Blessed are they whose eyes are only and altogether on the Crucified. The older I grow the more sure I am of this, that we must have done with self in all forms and see Jesus only if we would be at peace. Was John Bunyan wrong? Certainly not; he was describing things as they generally are. Was the old woman wrong? No, she was perfectly right: she was describing things as they ought to be, and as I wish they always were. Still, experience is not always as it ought to be, and much of the experience of Christians is not Christian experience. It is a fact which I lament, but, nevertheless, must admit, that a large number of persons, ere they come to the cross and lose their burden, go round about no end of a way, trying this plan and that plan, with but very slender success after all, instead of coming straightway to Christ just as they are, looking to him and finding light and life at once. How is it, then, that some are so long in getting to Christ?

I answer, first, in some cases it is *ignorance*. Perhaps there is no subject upon which men are so ignorant as the gospel. Is it not preached in hundreds of places? Yes, thank God, it is, and illustrated in no end of books; but still men come not at it so; neither hearing nor reading can of themselves discover the gospel. It needs the teaching of the Holy Spirit, or else men still remain in ignorance as to this simplicity—this simplicity of salvation by faith. Men are in the dark, and do not know the way; and so they run hither and thither, and oftentimes go round about to find a Saviour who is ready there and then to bless them. They cry, "Oh that I knew where I might find him!" when, if they did but understand the truth, his salvation is nigh them, "in their mouth and in their heart." If with their heart they will believe on the Lord Jesus, and with their mouth make confession of him, they shall be saved there and then.

In many cases, too, men are hindered by *prejudice*. People are brought up to the belief that salvation must be through ceremonies; and if they get driven out of that they still conclude that it must certainly be in some measure by their works. Numbers of people have learned a sort of half-and-half gospel, part law and part grace, and they are in a thick fog about salvation. They know that redemption has something to do with Christ, but it is much of a mixture with them; they do not quite see that it is all Christ or no Christ. They have a notion that we are saved by grace, but they do not yet see that salvation must be of grace from top to bottom; they fail to see that in order that salvation may be of grace it must be received by faith and not through the works of the law, nor by priestcraft, nor by any rites and ceremonies whatsoever. Being brought up to believe that surely there is something for them to do, it is long before they can get into the clear, blessed sunlight of the word, where the child of God sees Christ and finds liberty. "Believe and live" is a foreign language to a soul which is persuaded that its own works are in a measure to win eternal life.

With many, indeed, the hindrance lies in downright *bad teaching*. The teaching that is too common nowadays is very dangerous. The service makes no distinction between saint and sinner. Certain prayers are used every day which are meant for saints and sinners too—ready-made clothes, made to fit everybody, and fitting nobody at all. These prayers suit neither saint nor sinner, thoroughly beautiful as they are and grand as they are; but they bring up people under the notion and delusion that they are somewhere in a condition between being saved and being lost,—not actually lost, certainly, but yet not quite saints— they are betweenites, mongrels—a sort of Samaritans that fear the Lord and serve other gods, and who hope to be saved by an amalgam of grace and works. It is hard to bring men to grace alone and faith alone: they will stand with one foot on the sea, and the other foot on the land. Much of teaching goes to buoy them up in the notion that there is something in man and something to be done by him, and hence they do not learn in their own souls that they must be saved by Christ, and not by themselves.

Besides that, there is *the natural pride of the human heart.* We do not like to be saved by charity, we must have a finger in it. We get pushed into a corner; farther and farther are we driven away from self-confidence, but we hang on by our teeth, if we cannot find a hold by any other means. With awful desperation we trust in ourselves. We will cling by our eyelashes to the semblance of self-confidence: we will not give up carnal confidence if it be possible to hold it. Then comes in, with our pride, *opposition to God;* for the human heart does not love God, and it frequently shows its opposition by opposing him about the plan of salvation. The enmity of the unrenewed heart is not displayed by actual open sin in all cases, for many by their very bringings-up have been made to be moral, but they hate God's plan of grace, and grace alone, and here their gall and bitterness begin to work. How they will writhe in their seats if the minister preaches divine sovereignty; they hate the text "He will have mercy on whom he will have mercy, and he will have compassion on whom he will have compassion." They talk of the rights of fallen men, and of all being treated alike; and when it comes to sovereignty, and God's manifesting his grace according to his own absolute will, they cannot endure it. If they tolerate God at all it shall not be on the throne; if they acknowledge his existence, yet not as King of kings and Lord of lords who does as he wills, and has a right to pardon whom he reserves, and to leave the guilty, if so it pleases him, to perish in their guiltiness, rejecting the Saviour. Ah, the heart loves not God as God, as revealed in Scripture, but makes a god unto itself, and cries, "These be thy gods, O Israel."

In some instances the struggle of the heart in getting to Christ, I have no doubt, arises from *a singularity of mental conformation,* and such cases ought to be looked upon as exceptions, and by no means regarded as rules. Now take, for instance, the case of John Bunyan, to which we have referred. If you read "Grace Abounding," you will find that, for five years or more, he was the subject of the most fearful despair,—tempted by Satan, tempted by his own self, always raising difficulties against himself; and it was long, long, long before he could come to the cross and find peace. But then, dear friend, it is to the last degree improbable that either you or I will ever turn out John Bunyans. We may become tinkers, but we shall never write a Pilgrim's Progress. We might imitate him in his poverty, but we are not likely to emulate him in his genius: a man with such an imagination, full of wondrous dreams, is not born every day, and when he does come, his inheritance of brain is not all a gain in the direction of a restful life. When Bunyan's imagination had been purified and sanctified, its masterly productions were seen in his marvellous allegories; but while, as yet, he had not been renewed and reconciled to God, with such a mind, so strangely formed, so devoid of all education, and brought up as he had been in the roughest society, he was dowered with a fearful heritage. That marvellous fancy would have wrought him wondrous woe if it had not been controlled by the divine Spirit. Do you wonder that, in coming to the day, those eyes which had been veiled in such dense darkness could scarcely bear the light, and that the man should think the darkness all the darker when the light began to shine upon him? Bunyan was one by himself; not the rule, but the exception. Now, you, dear friend, may be an odd person. Very likely you are; and I can sympathize with you, for I am odd enough myself; but do not lay down a law that everybody else must be odd too. If you and I did happen to go round by the back ways, do not let us think that everybody ought to follow our bad example. Let us be very thankful that some people's minds are less twisted and gnarled than ours, and do not let us set up our experience as a standard for other people. No doubt difficulties may arise from an extraordinary quality of mind with which God may have gifted some, or a depression of spirit natural to others, and these may make them peculiar as long as they live.

Besides, there are some who are kept from coming to Christ through remarkable *assaults of Satan*. You remember the story of the child whom his father would bring to Jesus, but "as he was a coming the devil threw him down and tare him." The evil spirit knew that his time was short, and he must soon be expelled from his victim, and therefore he cast him on the ground, and made him wallow in epilepsy, and left him half dead. So does Satan with many men. He sets upon them with all the brutality of his fiendish nature, and expends his malice upon them, because he fears that they are about to escape from his service, and he will no longer be able to tyrannise over them. As Watts says—

> " He worries whom he can't devour,
> With a malicious joy."

Now, if some come to Christ, and the devil is not permitted to assail them, if some come to Christ, and there is nothing strange about their experience, if some come to Christ, and pride and opposition have been conquered in their nature, if some come to Christ, and they are not ignorant, but well instructed, and readily see the light, let us rejoice that it is so. It is of such that I am now about to speak somewhat more at length.

II. It is admitted as an undoubted fact that many are much troubled in coming to Christ; but now, secondly, THIS IS NOT AT ALL ESSENTIAL TO A REAL, SAVING COMING TO THE LORD JESUS CHRIST. I mention this because I have known Christian men distressed in heart because they fear that they came to Christ too easily. They have half imagined, as they looked back, that they could not have been converted at all, because their conversion was not attended with such agony and torment of mind as others speak of.

I would first remark, that *it is very hard to see how despairing feelings can be essential to salvation.* Look for a minute. Can it be possible that unbelief can help a soul to faith? Is it not certain that the anguish which many experience before they come to Christ arises from the fact of their unbelief? They do not trust,—they say they cannot trust; and so they are like the troubled sea which cannot rest. Their mind is tossed to and fro, and vexed sorely through unbelief; is this a foundation for holy trust? It would seem to me the oddest thing in all the world that unbelief should be a preparation for faith. How can it be that to sow the ground with thistle-seed should make it more ready for the good corn? Are fire and sword helpers to national prosperity? Is deadly poison an assistance to health? I do not understand it. It seems to me to be far better for the soul to believe the word of God at once, and far more likely to be a genuine work when the soul convinced of sin accepts the Saviour. Here is God's way of salvation, and he demands that I do trust his dear Son, who died for sinners. I perceive that Christ is worthy to be trusted, for he is the Son of God, so that his sacrifice must be able to put away my sin; I perceive also that he laid down his life in the room, place, and stead of his people, and therefore I heartily trust him. God bids me trust him, and I do trust him without any further question. If Jesus Christ satisfies God, he certainly satisfies me; and, asking no further question, I come and trust myself with him. Does not this kind of action appear to have about it all that can be needful? Can it possibly be that a raging, raving despair can ever be helpful towards saving faith? I do not see it. I cannot think it. Some have been beaten about with most awful thoughts. They have supposed that God could not possibly forgive them; they have imagined that, even if he could pardon them he would not, since they were not his elect, nor his redeemed. Though they have seen the gospel invitation written in letters of love: "Come unto me all ye that labour, and are heavy laden, and I will give you rest," they dare to question whether they should find rest if they did come, and they invent suspicions and surmises, some of them amounting even to blasphemy against the character of God and the person of his Christ. That such people have been forgiven according to the riches of divine grace I do verily believe, but that their sinful thoughts ever helped them to obtain pardon I cannot imagine. That my own dark thoughts of God, which left many a scar upon my spirit, were washed away with all my other sins, I know: that there was ever any good in those things, or that I can look back upon them without shame and regret, is a thing I do not know. I cannot see of what particular service they could have been to anybody. Shall one bath of ink take out the stain of another? Can our sin be removed by our sinning more? It is impossible that sin could aid grace, and that the greatest of all sins, the sin of unbelief, should help towards faith.

Yet, once again, dear friends, *much of all this struggling and tumult within, which some have experienced, is the work of the devil,* as I have already said. Can it be essential to salvation for a man to be under the influence of Satan? Is it needful that the devil should come in to help Christ? Is it absolutely essential for the black fingers of the devil to be seen at work with the lily hands of the Redeemer? Impossible. That is not my judgment of the work of Satan; nor will it, I think, be yours if you will look at it. If you never were driven either to blasphemy or despair by Satan, thank God you never were. You would have gained nothing by it; you would have been a serious loser. Let no man imagine that if he had been the prey of tormenting suggestions his conversion would have more marks of truth about it: no mistake can be more groundless. It cannot be that the devil can be of any service to anyone among you. He must do you damage, and nothing but damage. Every blow he strikes hurts but does not heal. Mr. Bunyan himself says, when he speaks of Christian fighting with Apollyon, that, though he won the victory, he was no gainer by it. A man had better go many miles round about, over hedge and ditch, sooner than once come into conflict with Apollyon. All that is essential to conversion is found in the simpler way of coming at once to Jesus, and as to all else we must face it if it comes, but certainly not look for it. It is easy to see how Satanic temptation hampers, and how it keeps men in bondage when otherwise they might be at liberty, but what good it can do in itself it would be hard to tell.

Once again, *many instances prove that all this law work, and doubting and fearing, and despairing, and being tormented of Satan, are not essential, because there are scores and hundreds of Christians who came at once to Christ, as these two blind men did, and to this very day know very little about those things.* I could, if it were proper, call upon brethren who are around me at this moment who would tell you that, when I have been preaching the experience of those who come to Christ with difficulty, they have been glad that it should be preached, but they have felt, "We know nothing of all this in our own experience." Taught from their very youth the way of God, trained by godly parents, they came under the influences of the Holy Spirit very early in life, they heard that Jesus Christ could save them, they knew that they wanted saving, and they just went to him, I was about to say, almost as naturally as they went to their mother or their father when they were in need: they trusted the Saviour, and they found peace at once. Several of the honoured leaders of this church came to the Lord in this simple manner. Only yesterday I was greatly pleased with several that I saw who confessed faith in Jesus in a way which charmed me, and yet about their Christian experience there was little trace of terrible burns and scars. They heard the gospel, they saw the suitability of it to their case, and they accepted it there and then, and entered immediately into peace and joy. Now, we do not tell you that there are a few such plain cases, but we assert boldly that we know hosts of like instances, and that there are thousands of God's most honoured servants who are walking before him in holiness, and are eminently useful, whose experience is as simple as A B C. Their whole story might be summed up in the verse,—

> "I came to Jesus, as I was,
> Weary and worn and sad:
> I found in him a resting-place,
> And he has made me glad."

I will go yet further and assure you that many of those who give the best evidence that they are renewed by grace cannot tell you the day in which they were saved, and cannot attribute their conversion to any one sermon or to any one text of Scripture, or to any one event in life. We dare not doubt their conversion for their lives prove its truth. You may have many trees in your garden of which you must admit that you don't know when they were planted; but, if you get plenty of fruit

from them, you are not very particular about the date of their striking
root. I am acquainted with several persons who do not know their own
age. I was talking to one the other day who thought herself ten years older
than I found her out to be. I did not tell her that she was not alive,
because she did not know her birthday. If I had told her so, she would
have laughed at me ; and yet there are some who fancy that they cannot be converted because they do not know the date of their conversion.
Oh, if you are trusting the Saviour,—if he is all your salvation and
all your desire, and if your life is affected by your faith, so that you
bring forth the fruits of the Spirit, you need not worry about times and
seasons.

Thousands in the fold of Jesus can declare that they are in it, but
the day that they passed through the gate is totally unknown to them.
Thousands there are who came to Christ, not in the darkness of the
night, but in the brightness of the day, and these cannot talk of weary
waitings and watchings, though they can sing of free grace and dying
love. They came joyously home to their Father's house : the sadness
of repentance was sweetened with the delight of faith, which came sim-
ultaneously with repentance to their hearts. I know it is so. We tell
you but the simple truth. Many young people are brought to the
Saviour to the sound of sweet music. Many also of another class,
namely, the simple-minded, come in like manner. We might all wish
to belong to that class. Some professors would be ashamed to be
thought simple-minded, but I would glory in it. Too many of the
doubting, critical order are great puzzle-makers, and great fools for
their pains. The childlike ones drink the milk while these folks are
analyzing it. They seem every night to take themselves to pieces
before they go to bed, and it is very hard for them in the morning to
put themselves together again. To some minds the hardest thing
in the world is to believe a self-evident truth. They must always, if
they can, make a dust and a mist, and puzzle themselves, or else they
are not happy. In fact, they are never sure till they are uncertain, and
never at ease till they are disturbed. Blessed are those who believe
that God cannot lie, and are quite sure it must be so if God has said
it ; these cast themselves upon Christ whether they sink or swim, because
if Christ's salvation is God's way of saving man, it must be the right
way, and they accept it. Many, I say, have thus come to Christ.

Now, proceeding a step farther, *there are all the essentials of salvation
in the simple, pleasant, happy way of coming to Jesus just as you are;*
for what are the essentials ? The first is *repentance,* and these dear
souls, though they feel no remorse, yet hate the sin they once loved.
Though they know no dread of hell, yet they feel a dread of sin,
which is a great deal better. Though they have never stood shivering
under the gallows, yet the crime is more dreadful to them than the
doom. They have been taught by God's Spirit to love righteousness
and seek after holiness, and this is the very essence of repentance.
Those who thus come to Christ have certainly obtained true *faith.*
They have no experience which they could trust in, but they are all
the more fully driven to rest in what Christ has felt and done. They
rest not in their own tears, but in Christ's blood; not in their own
emotions, but in Christ's pangs ; not in their consciousness of ruin,

but **in** the certainty that Christ has come to **save** all those that trust him. They have faith of the purest kind.

And see, too, how certainly they have *love*. " Faith works by love," and they show it. They often seem to have more love at the first than those who come so dreadfully burdened and tempest-tossed ; for, in the calm quiet of their minds, they get a fairer view of the beauties of the Saviour, and they burn with love to him, and they commence to serve him, while others, as yet, are having their wounds healed, and are trying to make their broken bones rejoice. I am not wishing to depreciate a painful experience, but I am only wanting to show, as to this second class, that their simple coming to Christ, as the blind men came, their simply believing that he could give them sight, is not one whit inferior to the other, and has in it all the essentials of salvation.

For, next, notice that *the gospel command implies in itself nothing of the kind which some have experienced.* What are we bidden to preach to men—" Be dragged about by the devil, and you shall be saved" ? No, but " Believe in the Lord Jesus Christ, and thou shalt be saved." What is my commission at this time? To say to you, " Despair, and ye shall be saved" ? No, verily; but " Believe, and you shall be saved." Are we to come here and say, " Torture yourself; mangle your heart, scourge your spirit, grind your very soul to powder in desperation"? No, but " Believe in the infinite goodness and mercy of God in the person of his dear Son, and come and trust him." That is the gospel command. It is put in various forms. This is one— " Look unto me, and be ye saved, all the ends of the earth." Now, if I were to come and say, " Tear your eyes out," that would not be the the gospel, would it? No, but " Look." The gospel does not say, " Cry your eyes out," but " Look." And it does not say, " Blind your eyes with a hot iron." No, but " Look, look, look." It is just the very opposite of anything like remorse, despair, and blasphemous thought. It is just " Look." Then it is put in another shape. We are told to take of the water of life freely ; we are bidden to drink of the eternal spring of love and life. What are we told to do? To make this water of life scalding hot? No. We are to drink it as it freely flows out of the fountain. Are we to make it drip after the manner of the Inquisition, a drop at a time, and to lie under it, and feel the perpetual drip of a scanty trickling? Nothing of the sort. We are just to step down to the fountain, and drink, and be contented therewith, for it will quench our thirst. What is the gospel again? Is it not to eat the bread of heaven ? " Eat ye that which is good." There is the gospel banquet, and we are to compel men to come in ; and what are they to do when they come in? Silently to look on while others eat? Stand and wait till they feel more hungry? Try forty days' fasting, like Dr. Tanner ? Nothing of the sort. You might think this to be the gospel by the way some people preach and act, but it is not so. You are to feast on Christ at once ; you need not fast till you turn yourself into a living skeleton, and then come to Christ. I am sent with no such message as that, but this is my word of good cheer : " Hearken diligently unto me, and eat ye that which is good, and let your soul delight itself in fatness. Ho, every one that thirsteth, come ye to the waters, and he that hath no money ; let him come, buy wine and milk, without money and without price." Freely take what God freely gives, and simply trust the Saviour. Is not that the gospel? Well, then, why should any of you say, "I cannot trust Christ, because I don't feel this, and don't feel that"? Do I not assure you solemnly that I have known of many who have come to Christ just as they were—who have never undergone those horrible feelings which are so much spoken of, and yet have been most truly saved? Come as you are. Do not try to make a righteousness out of your unrighteousness, or a confidence out of your unbelief, or a Christ out of your blasphemies, as some seem to do; nor dote so foolishly as to imagine that despair may be a ground of hope. It cannot be. You are to get out of self, and into Christ, and there you will be safe. As the blind man said, when Christ asked him, "Believest thou that I am able to do this?" so are you to say unto him, "Yea, Lord." Trust yourself with your Saviour, and he is your Saviour.

III. I conclude with one more observation, that THOSE PERSONS WHO ARE PRIVILEGED TO COME TO JESUS CHRIST SOFTLY, PLEASANTLY, AND HAPPILY, ARE NOT LOSERS. They do lose something, certainly; but there is not much in it. They lose somewhat of the picturesque, and they have the less to tell. When a man has had a long series of trials to drive him out of himself, and at last he comes to Christ, like a wrecked vessel tugged into port, he has a deal to talk of and write about, and perhaps he thinks it interesting to be able to tell it; and, if he can tell it to God's glory, it is quite proper that he should. Many of these stories are found in biographies, because they are the incidents which excite interest and make a life worth writing; but you must not conclude that all godly lives are of the same sort. Happy are those whose lives could not be written because they were so happy as to be uneventful. Some of the most favoured lives do not get written because there is nothing very picturesque about them. But I ask you this, when those blind men came to Christ just as they were, and said that they believed that he could open their eyes, and he did open their eyes, is there not as much *of Christ* in their story as there well could be? The men themselves are nowhere, but the healing Master is in the foreground. More detail might almost take away the peculiar prominence that he has in it all. There he stands, the blessed, glorious opener of the eyes of the two blind men; there he stands alone, and his name is glorious! There was a woman who had spent all her substance upon physicians, and was nothing better, but rather grew worse. She had a long tale to tell of the various doctors she had been to; but I do not know that the narrative of her many disappointments would glorify the Lord Jesus one bit more than when these two blind men could say, "We heard of him, and we went to him, and he opened our eyes. We never spent a halfpenny upon doctors. We went straight away to Jesus, just as we were, and all he said to us was, 'Do you think that I can do it?' and we said, 'Yes, we believe you can,' and he opened our eyes directly; and it was all done." Oh, if my experience should ever stand in my Master's light, perish my best experience! Let Christ be first, last, midst; do you not say so, my brethren? If you, poor sinner, come to Christ at once, with nothing about you whatever that you ever can talk of,—if you are just a nobody coming to the ever-blessed Everybody —if you are a mere nothing coming to him who is the All-in-all; if you are a lump of sin and misery, a great vacuum, nothing but an emptiness that never need be thought of any more, if you will come and lose yourselves in his infinitely glorious grace—this will be all that is wanted. It seems to me that you will lose nothing by the fact that there is not so much of the picturesque and the sensational in your experience. There will be, at least, this grand sensation—lost in self but saved in Jesus, glory be to his name.

Perhaps you may suppose that persons who come thus gently lose something by way of evidence afterwards. " Ah," said one to me, " I could almost wish sometimes that I had been an open offender, that I might see the change in my character; but, having been always moral from my youth up, I am not always able to see any distinct mark of a change." Ah, let me tell you, friends, that this form of evidence is of small use in times of darkness, for if the devil cannot say to a man, " You have not changed your life "—for there are some that he would not have the impudence to say that to, since the change is too manifest for him to deny it—he says, "You changed your actions, but your heart is still the same. You turned from a bold, honest sinner to be a hypocritical, canting professor. That is all you have done; you have given up open sin because your strong passions declined, or you thought you would like another way of sinning; and now you are only making a false profession, and living far from what you should do." Very little consolation is to be got even out of the change that conversion works when once the arch-enemy becomes our accuser. In fact, it comes to this: however you come to Christ you can never place any confidence in how you came. Your confidence must always rest in him you came to—that is, in Christ—whether you come to him flying, or running, or walking. If you get to Jesus you are all right, anyhow: but it is not how you come, it is whether you come *to him*. Have you come to Jesus? Do you come to Jesus? If you have come, and you doubt whether you have come, come over again. Never quarrel with Satan about whether you are a Christian. If he says you are a sinner reply to him, " So I am, but Jesus Christ came into the world to save sinners, and I will begin again." He is an old lawyer, you know, and very cunning, and he knows how to baffle us, for we do not understand things so well as he does. He has been these thousands of years at the trade of trying to make Christians doubt their interest in Christ, and he understands it well. Never answer him. Refer him to your solicitor; tell him you have an Advocate on high who will answer him. Tell him you will fly away to Christ again; if you never went to Jesus before you will go now, and if you have been before you will go again. That is the way to end the quarrel. As to evidences, they are fine things in fine weather, but when the tempest is out wise men let evidences go. The best evidence a man can have that he is saved is that he is still clinging to Christ.

Lastly, some may suppose that those who come gently to Christ may lose a good deal of adaptation for after usefulness, because they will not be able to sympathize with those who are in deep perplexity, and in awful straits when they are coming to Christ. Ah, well, there are enough of us who *can* sympathize with such; and I do not know that everybody is bound to sympathize with everybody in every respect. I remember mentioning one day to a man who had considerable property that his poor minister had a large family and could scarcely keep a coat on his back. I said I wondered how some Christian men who profited under the ministry of such a man did not supply his wants; he answered that he thought it was a good thing for ministers to be poor, because they could sympathize with the poor. I said " Yes, yes, but then, don't you see, there ought to be one or two that are not poor to sympathize with those who are rich." I would give them turn about, certainly, and let the poor pastor now and then have the power to sympathize with both classes. He did not seem to see my argument, but I think there is a good deal in it. It is a great mercy to have some brethren around us who, by their painful experience, can sympathize with those who have been through that pain; but do you not think it is a great mercy to have others who, through not having undergone that experience, can sympathize with others who have not undergone it? Is it not useful to have some who can say, "Well, dear heart, don't be troubled because the great dog of hell did not howl at you. If you have entered the gate calmly and quietly, and Christ has received you, do not be troubled because you are not barked at by the devil, for I, too, came to Jesus just as gently and safely and sweetly as you have done"? Such a testimony will comfort the poor soul; and so, if you lose the power to sympathize one way, you will gain the power to sympathize in another; and there will be no great loss after all.

To sum up all in one, I would that every man and woman and child here would come and trust the Lord Jesus Christ. It seems to me to be such a matchless plan of salvation, for Christ to take human sin and to suffer in the sinner's stead, and for us to have nothing to do but just to accept what Christ has done, and to trust ourselves wholly with him. He that would not be saved by such a plan as this deserves to perish; and so he must. Was there ever so sweet, so sure, and so plain a gospel? It is a joy to preach it. Will you have it? Dear souls, will you not yield to be nothing and have Jesus to be all in all?

God grant that none of us may reject this way of grace, this open way, this safe way. Come, linger no longer. The Spirit and the bride say " Come." Lord, draw them by the love of Jesus. Amen.

Honey From a Lion

"But not as the offence, so also is the free gift. For if through the offence of one many be dead, much more the grace of God, and the gift by grace, which is by one man, Jesus Christ, hath abounded unto many."—Romans v. 15.

THIS text affords many openings for controversy. It can be made to bristle with difficulties. For instance,—there might be a long discussion as to the manner in which the fall of Adam can justly be made to affect the condition of his posterity. When this is settled there might arise a question as to the exact way in which Adam's fault is connected with ourselves—whether by imputation of its sin, or in what other form; and then there might be further dispute as to the limit of the evil resulting from our first parents' offence, and the full meaning of the fall, original sin, natural depravity, and so forth. There would be another splendid opportunity for a great battle over the question of the extent of the redeeming work of the Lord Jesus Christ; whether it covers, as to persons, the whole area of the ruin of the Fall; whether, in fact, full atonement has been made for all mankind or only for the elect. It would be easy in this way to set up a thorn-hedge, and keep the sheep out of the pasture; or, to use another metaphor, to take up so much time in pelting each other with the stones as to leave the fruit untasted. I have, at this time, neither the inclination nor the mental strength either to suggest or to remove the difficulties, which are so often the amusement of unpractical minds. I feel more inclined to chime in with that ancient father of the church who declined controversy in a wise and explicit manner. He had been speaking concerning the things of God and found himself at length confounded by a certain clamorous disputant, who shouted again and again, "Hear me! Hear me!" "No," said the father, "I will not hear *you*, nor shall you hear *me*; but we will both be quiet and hear what our Lord Jesus Christ has to say." So we will not at this time listen to this side nor to that; but we will bow our ear to hear what the Scripture itself hath to say apart from all the noise of sect and party. My object shall be to find out in the text that which is practically of use to us, that which may save the unconverted, that which may comfort and build up those of us who are brought into a state of reconciliation with God; for I have of late been so often shut up in my sick chamber that when I do come forth I must be more than ever eager for fruit to the glory of God. We shall not, therefore, dive into the deeps with the hope of finding pearls, for these could not feed hungry men; but we will navigate the surface of the sea, and hope that some favouring wind will bear us to the desired haven with a freight of corn wherewith to supply the famishing. May the Holy Spirit bless the teaching of this hour to the creation and nourishment of saving faith.

I. The first observation from the text is this—THE APPOINTED WAY OF OUR SALVATION IS BY THE FREE GIFT OF GOD. We were ruined by the Fall, but we are saved by a free gift. The text tells us that "the grace of God, and the gift by grace, which is by one man, Jesus Christ, hath abounded unto many." "Where sin abounded, grace did much more abound." "Grace reigns through righteousness unto eternal life by Jesus Christ our Lord." Although this doctrine is well known, and is taught in our synagogues every Sabbath day, yet this grand essential truth is often enough forgotten or ignored, so that it had need be repeated again and again. I could wish that every time the clock struck it said, "By grace are ye saved." I could wish that there were a trumpet voice ringing out at day-break both on sea and land, over the whole round globe the words, "By grace are ye saved." As Martin Luther said of a certain other truth so say I of this, "You so constantly forget it that I feel inclined to take the Bible and beat it about your head, that you may feel it and keep it in remembrance." Men do not naturally love the doctrine of grace, and therefore they cast it out of their minds as much as possible. The larger portion of mankind do not believe that salvation is of grace : another part of them profess to believe it, but do not understand its meaning ; and many who do understand it have never yielded to it or embraced it. Happy are they who belong to the remnant according to the election of grace, for they know right well the joyful sound, and they walk in the light of the glory of the grace of God which is in Christ Jesus.

Observe, that salvation is a free gift, that is to say, it is bestowed upon men by God *without regard to any merit, supposed or real.* Grace has to do with the guilty. Mercy in the very nature of things is not a fit gift for the righteous and deserving, but for the undeserving and sinful. When God deals out to men his gracious salvation they are regarded by him as lost and condemned, and he treats them as persons who have no claim upon him whatsoever, to whom nothing but his free favour can bring deliverance. He saves them, not because he perceives that they have done anything that is good, or have hopeful traits of character, or form resolutions to aspire to something better; but simply because he is merciful, and delights to exercise his grace, and manifest his free favour and infinite love. It is according to the nature of God to pity the miserable and forgive the guilty, "for he is good, and his mercy endureth for ever." God has a reason for saving men; but that reason does not lie in man's merit in any degree whatever. This is clear from the fact that he often begins his work of grace upon those who can least of all be credited with goodness. It was said of our Lord, "This man receiveth sinners," and the saying was most emphatically true. Sovereign grace selects such as Rahab the harlot, and Manasseh the persecutor, and Saul of Tarsus, the mad zealot against

Christ : such as these have been seized upon by grace, and arrested in infinite love, that in them the Lord might manifest the power and plenitude of his mercy. Salvation is a work which is begun by the pure, unpurchased, free favour of God, and in the same spirit it is carried on and perfected. Pure grace, which lays the foundation, also brings forth the topstone.

Salvation is also brought to men *irrespective of any merit which God foresees will be in man.* Foresight of the existence of grace cannot be the cause of grace. God himself does not foresee that there will be any good thing in any man, except what he foresees that he will put there. What is the reason, then, why he determines that he will put it there? That reason, so far as we are informed, is this, " He will have mercy on whom he will have mercy." The Lord determines to display his love, and set on active work his attribute of grace, therefore doth he save men according to the good pleasure of his will. If there be salvation given to men upon the foresight of what they are yet to be, it is clear it is a matter of works and debt, and not of grace; but the Scripture is most decided that it is not of works, but of unmingled grace, for saith the apostle, " If by grace, then is it no more of works : otherwise grace is no more grace. But if it be of works, then is it no more grace : otherwise work is no more work." Our text is express that salvation is " the free gift," and that it comes to us by " the grace of God, and the gift by grace, which is by one man, Jesus Christ."

I go a little further in trying to explain how salvation is a free gift, by saying that it is given *without reference to conditions which imply any desert.* But I hear one murmur, " God will not give grace to men who do not repent." I answer, God gives men grace to repent, and no man ever repents till first grace is given him by which he is led to repentance. " God will not give his grace to those who do not believe," says one. I reply, God gives grace to men by which they are moved to believe, and it is through the grace of God that they are brought into the faith of Jesus Christ. You may say, if you please, that repentance and faith are conditions of salvation, and I will not quarrel with you ; but please remember that they are not conditions in the sense of deserving anything of God. They may be conditions of receiving, but they are not conditions of purchasing, for salvation is without money and without price. We are expressly told that salvation " is of faith, that it might be by grace ": for faith is not to be numbered with works of the law, to which the idea of merit may be attached. Faith is far as the poles asunder from claiming anything of God by way of debt. Faith comes as a poor, undeserving thing, and simply trusts the free mercy of God. It never attempts to wear the crown, or grasp a particle of praise. The believer never can be a boaster, for boasting is excluded by the law, of faith. If a Christian should begin to boast, it would be because his believing is failing, and his evil nature is coming to the front ; for faith is of all graces most self-denying; her song is always, *Non nobis Domine*, " Not unto us, but unto thy name give praise." While, therefore, the word of God assures us that except we repent we shall all likewise perish, and that if we believe not in Jesus Christ we shall die in our sins, it would have us at the same time know that there is no merit in repenting or believing, but grace reigns in God's acceptance of these graces. We are not to regard the requirement of faith, repentance, and confession of sin as at all militating against the fulness and freeness of divine grace, since, in the first place, both repentance, faith, and true confession of sin are all gifts of grace, and, in the next place, they have no merit in themselves, being only such things as honest men should render when they know that they have erred and are promised forgiveness. To be sorry for my sin is no recompense for having sinned; and to believe God to be true is no work for which I may demand a reward; if, then, I am saved through faith, it is of the pure mercy of God, and of that alone that pardon comes to me.

Beloved, so far is God from giving salvation to men as a matter of reward and debt, and therefore bestowing it only upon the good and excellent, that *he is pleased to bestow that salvation over the head of sin and in the teeth of rebellion*. As I said before, mercy and grace are for the sinful, for none others need them; and God's grace comes to us when we are far off by wicked works. "God commendeth his love toward us, in that, while we were yet sinners, Christ died for us." Free grace breaks forth like a mighty flood, and sweeps in torrents over the hills of our transgressions, rising above the high alps of our presumptuous sins. Twenty cubits upward doth this sea of grace prevail till the tops of the mountains of iniquity are covered. The Lord passeth by transgression, iniquity, and sin, and remembereth not the iniquity of his people, because he delighteth in mercy. Almsgiving needs a pauper, and grace needs a sinner. There is no opportunity for forgiveness where there is no offence. If men are meritorious how can God be gracious to them? In such a case it will be enough for him to be just. When good works can put in a valid claim peace and heaven can be obtained by the rules of debt; but since it is clear that eternal life is the gift of pure favour, you need not marvel when I say that grace comes to men leaping over the mountains of their iniquities. Abounding mercy delights to blot out abounding sin, and it will never lack for opportunity to do its pleasure. There is no lack of occasions for grace in this poor fallen world, and of all the places where there is most room I know of one spot not far from here where there is a grand opportunity for infinite mercy and superabounding grace to exercise their power. Here is the spot—it is this treacherous, guilty heart of mine. I think, my brother, you know of another spot that is very like it; and you, my sister, too, can say, "Wondrous mercy! Sure there is room for all its heights and depths to be shown in this sinful soul of mine." Ay, and it will be shown, too, if you can but look for it through Christ Jesus; for it is the delight of God's grace to flow into unlikely places: mercy is the glory of God, and he loves to bestow it on those who least deserve it.

We are saved by grace, free grace, pure grace, grace without regard to merit or to the possibility of such a thing, and *many of us have been saved by grace of the most abounding and extraordinary sort*. Some of us will be prodigies of divine love, miracles of mercy, to be wondered at throughout eternity: we shall be set up in heaven as monuments for angels to gaze at, in which they shall see a display of the amazing goodness of the Lord. *Some of us*, I said; but I suppose that in each one of the redeemed there is some particular development of grace which will make him specially remarkable, so that the whole body of us, as one glorified church, shall be made known unto angels, and principalities, and powers, the manifold wisdom of God. Oh, what a revelation of grace and mercy will be seen when all the blood-washed race shall gather safely around the eternal throne, and sing their hallelujahs unto him that loved them and washed them from their sins in his own blood.

Note one thing more concerning this plan of salvation, that *all this grace comes to us through the one man Jesus Christ.* I sometimes hear people talking about a "one man ministry." I know what they mean, but I know also that I am saved by a one man ministry, even by one who trod the winepress alone, and of the people there was none with him. I was lost by a one man ministry, when father Adam fell in Eden; but I was saved by a one man ministry, when the blessed Lord Jesus Christ bore my sin in his own body on the tree. O matchless ministry of love, when the Lord from heaven came into the world and took upon himself our nature, and became in all respects human, and being found in fashion as a man, was obedient to death, even the death of the cross! It is through the one man, Christ Jesus, that all the grace of God comes streaming down to all the chosen. Mercy flows to no man save through the one appointed channel, Jesus the Son of man. Get away from Christ, and you leave the highway of God's everlasting love; pass this door, and you shall find no entrance into life. You must drink from this conduit-pipe, or you must thirst for ever, and ask in vain for a drop of water to cool your parched tongue. "In him dwelleth all the fulness of the Godhead bodily." All the infinite mercy of God and love of God —and God himself is love—is concentrated in the person of the well-beloved Son of the Highest, and unto him be glory for ever. Sing unto him, ye angels! Chant his praise, ye redeemed! For by the one man Christ Jesus the whole company of the elect have been delivered from the wrath to come, to the praise of the glory of the grace of God.

Thus I have tried to set before you God's way of salvation.

II. Starting aside, as it may seem, from the current of our thoughts, but only with the view of coming back to it with a forcible argument, we next note that IT IS CERTAIN THAT GREAT EVILS HAVE COME TO US BY THE FALL. Paul speaks in this text of ours of the "offence," which word may be read the "Fall," which was caused by the stumbling of our father Adam. Our fall in Adam is a type of the salvation which is in Christ Jesus, but the type is not able completely to set forth all the work of Christ: hence the apostle says, "But not as the offence, so also is the free gift. For if through the offence of one many be dead, much more the grace of God, and the gift by grace, which is by one man, Jesus Christ, hath abounded unto many." It is certain, then, that we were heavy losers by the offence of the first father and head of our race. I am not going into details and particulars, but it is clear that we have *lost the garden of Eden* and all its delights, privileges, and immunities, its communion with God, and its freedom from death. We have lost our first honour and health, and we have become the subjects of pain and weakness, suffering and death: this is the effect of the Fall. A desert now howls where otherwise a garden would have smiled. Through the sin of Adam we have been born under conditions which are far from being desirable, heirs to *a heritage of sorrow.* Our griefs have been alleviated by the bounty of God, but still we are not born under such conditions as might have been ours had Adam remained in his integrity and kept his first estate. We came into the world with *a bias towards evil.* Those of us who have any knowledge of our own nature must confess that there is in us a strong tendency towards sin, which is mixed up with our very being. This is not derived solely from faults of education, or from the imitation of others ; but there is a bent within us in the wrong direction, and this has been there from our birth. Alas! that it should be so ; but so it is. In addition to having this tendency to sin, we are made *liable to death*—nay, not liable alone, but we are sure in due time to bow our heads beneath the fatal stroke. Two only of the human race have escaped death, but the rest have left their bodies here to moulder back into mother earth, and unless the Lord cometh speedily, we expect that the same thing will happen to these bodies of ours. While we live we know that the *sweat of our brow* must pay the price of our bread ; we know that our children must be born with pangs and travail ; we know that we our-selves must return to the dust from whence we are taken ; for dust we are, and unto dust must we return. O Adam, thou didst a sad day's work for us when thou didst hearken to the voice of thy wife and eat of the forbidden tree. The world has no more a Paradise anywhere, but everywhere it has the place of wailing and the field of the dead. Where can you go and not find traces of the first transgression in the sepulchre and its mouldering bones? Every field is fattened with the dust of the departed : every wave of the sea is tainted with atoms of the dead. Scarcely blows a March wind down our streets but it sweeps aloft the dust either of Cæsar or his slave, of ancient Briton, or modern Saxon ; for the globe is worm-eaten by death. Sin has scarred, and marred, and spoiled this creation by making it subject to vanity through its offence. Thus terrible evils have come to us by an act in which we had no hand : we were not in the Garden of Eden, we did not incite Adam to rebellion, and yet we have become sufferers through no deed of ours. Say what you will about it, the fact remains, and cannot be escaped from.

This sad truth leads me on to the one which is the essence of the text, and constitutes my third observation.

III. FROM THE FALL WE INFER THE MORE ABUNDANT CERTAINTY THAT SALVATION BY GRACE THROUGH CHRIST JESUS SHALL COME TO BELIEVERS. If all this mischief has happened to us through the fall of Adam why should not immense blessing flow to us by the work of Christ? Through Adam's transgression we lost Paradise, that is certain ; but if anything can be more certain we may with greater positiveness declare that the second Adam will restore the ruin of the first. If through the offence of one man many be dead, much more the grace of God and the gift by grace, which is by one man, Jesus Christ, shall abound and has abounded unto many. Settle in your minds, then, that the fall of Adam has wrought us great damage, and then be as much assured that the life, death, and resurrection of Christ, in which we had no hand whatever, must do us great service. Believing in Christ Jesus, it becomes beyond all measure sure to us that we are blessed in him, seeing that it is already certain that through the fall of Adam we have become subject to sorrow and death.

For, first, *this appears to be more delightful to the heart of God.* It must be fully according to his gracious nature that salvation should come to us through his Son. I can understand that God, having so arranged it that the human race should be regarded as one, and should stand or fall before him in one man, should carry out the arrangement to its righteous end, and allow the consequences of sin to fall upon succeeding generations of men : but yet I know that he takes no pleasure in the death of any, and finds no delight in afflicting mankind. When the first Adam transgressed it was inevitable that the consequences of his transgression should descend to his posterity, and yet I can imagine a perfectly holy mind questioning whether the arrangement would be carried out. I can conceive of angels saying one to another, " Will all men die through this entrance of sin into the world ? Can it be that the innumerable sons of Adam will all suffer from his disobedience ?" But I cannot imagine any question being raised about the other point, namely, the result of the work of our Lord Jesus. If God has so arranged it that in the second Adam men rise and live, it seems to me most gloriously consistent with his gracious nature and infinite love that it should come to pass that all who believe in Jesus should be saved through him. I cannot imagine angels hesitating and saying, " Christ has been born ; Christ has lived ; Christ has died ; these men have had nothing to do with that : will God save them for the sake of his Son ?" Oh, no, they must have felt, as they saw the babe born at Bethlehem, as they saw him living his perfect life and dying his atoning death, " God will bless those who are in Christ ; God will save Christ's people for Christ's sake." As for ourselves, we are sure that if the Lord executes judgment, which is his strange work, he will certainly carry out mercy, which is his delight. If he kept to the representative principle when it involved consequences which gave him no pleasure, we may be abundantly assured that he will keep to it now that it will involve nothing but good to those concerned in it. Here, then, is the argument,—" For if through the offence of one many be dead, much more the grace of God, and the gift by grace, which is by one man, Jesus Christ, hath abounded unto many."

This assurance becomes stronger still when we think that *it seems more inevitable that men should be saved by the death of Christ than that men should be lost by the sin of Adam.* It might seem possible that, after Adam had sinned, God might have said, " Notwithstanding this covenant of works, I will not lay this burden upon the children of Adam "; but it is not possible that after the eternal Son of God has become man, and has bowed his head to death, God should say, " Yet after all I will not save men for Christ's sake." Stand and look at the Christ upon the cross, and mark those wounds of his, and you will become absolutely certain that sin can be pardoned, nay, must be pardoned to those who are in Christ Jesus. Those flowing drops of blood demand with a voice that cannot be gainsaid that iniquity should be put away. If the voice of Abel crying from the ground was prevalent, how much more the blood of the Only-begotten Son of God, who through the eternal Spirit offered himself without spot ? It cannot be, O God, that thou shouldest despise or forget the sacrifice on Calvary. Grace must flow to sinners through the bleeding

Saviour, seeing that death came to men through their transgressing progenitor.

I do not know whether I shall get into the very soul of this argument as I desire, but to me it is very sweet to look at *the difference as to the causes of the two effects.* Look now at the occasion of our ruin,—" the offence of one." The one man transgresses, and you and I and all of us come under sin, sorrow, and death. What are we told is the fountain of these streams of woe ? The one action of our first parents. Far be it from me to say a word to depreciate the greatness of their crime, or to raise a question as to the justice of its consequences. I think no one can have a more decided opinion upon that point than I have ; for the offence was very great, and the principle which led to our participation in its results is a just one, and, what is more, is fraught with the most blessed after-consequences to fallen men, since it has left them a door of hope of their rising by the same method which led to their fall. Yet the sin which destroyed us was the transgression of a finite being, and cannot be compared in power with the grace of the infinite God; it was the sin of a moment, and therefore cannot be compared for force and energy with the everlasting purpose of divine love. If, then, the comparatively feeble fount of Adam's sin sends forth a flood which drowns the world in sorrow and death, what must be the boundless blessing poured forth from the infinite source of divine grace ? The grace of God is like his nature, omnipotent and unlimited. God hath not a measure of love, but he is love ; love to the uttermost dwells in him. God is not only gracious to this degree or to that, but he is gracious beyond measure; we read of " the exceeding riches of his grace." He is "the God of all grace," and his mercy is great above the heavens. Our largest conceptions fall far short of the lovingkindness and pity of God, for " his merciful kindness is great towards us." As high as the heavens are above the earth, so are his thoughts above our thoughts in the direction of grace. If, then, my brethren, the narrow fount which yielded bitter and poisonous waters has sufficed to slay the myriads of the human race, how much more shall the river of God which is full of water, even the river of the water of life, which proceedeth out of the throne of God and of the Lamb, supply life and bliss to every man that believeth in Christ Jesus ? Thus saith Paul, " For if by one man's offence death reigned by one ; much more they which receive abundance of grace and of the gift of righteousness shall reign in life by one, Jesus Christ." That is the argument of the text, and to me it seems to be a very powerful one, sufficient to dash out the very life of unbelief and enable every penitent man to say, " I see what I have lost in Adam, but I also see how much I obtain through Christ Jesus, my Lord, when I humbly yield myself to him."

Furthermore, I would have you note *the difference of the channels* by which the evil and the good were severally communicated to us. In each case it was "by one," but what a difference in the persons ! We fell through Adam, a name not to be pronounced without reverence, seeing he is the chief patriarch of the race, and the children should honour the parent : let us not think too little of the head of the human family. Yet what is the first Adam as compared with the second Adam ? He is but of the earth earthy, but the second man is the Lord from heaven. He was at best a mere man, but our Redeemer counts it not robbery to be equal with God. Surely, then, if Adam with that puny hand of his could pull down the house of our humanity, and hurl this ruin on our first estate, that greater man, who is also the Son of God, can fully restore us and bring back to our race the golden age. If one man could ruin by his fault, surely an infinitely greater man in whom dwelleth all the fulness of the Godhead bodily can restore us by the abounding grace of God.

And look, my brethren, what this man did. Adam commits *one* fault and spoils us; but Christ's works and achievements are not one, but many as the stars of heaven. Look at that life of obedience: it is like a crown set with all manner of priceless jewels: all the virtues are in it, and it is without flaw in any point. If one sinful action of our first covenant head destroys, shall not a whole life of holiness, on the part of our second covenant representative be accepted for us?

But what is more, Adam did but eat of the forbidden fruit, but our Lord Jesus died, pouring out his soul unto death, bearing the sin of his people upon himself. Such a death must have more force in it than the sad deed of Adam. Shall it not save us? Is there any comparison between the one act of rebellion in the garden and the matchless deed of superlative obedience upon the cross of Calvary which crowned a life of service? Am I sure that the act of disobedience has done me damage? Then I am much more certain that the glorious act of self-sacrifice must be able to save me, and I cast myself upon it without question or misgiving. The passion of God's Only-begotten must have in it infallible virtue for the remission of sin. Upon the perfect work of Jesus my soul hangs at this moment, without a suspicion of possible failure, and without the addition of the shadow of a confidence anywhere else. The good which may be supposed to be in man, his best words and holiest actions, are all to me as the small dust of the balance as to any title to the favour of God. My sole claim for salvation lies in that one man, the gift of God, who by his life and death has made atonement for my sin, but that one man, Christ Jesus, is a sure foundation, and a nail upon which we may hang all the weight of our eternal interests. I feel the more confidence in the certainty of salvation by Christ because of my firm persuasion of the dreadful efficacy of Adam's fall. Think awhile and it will seem strange, yet strangely true, that the hope of Paradise regained should be argued and justified by the fact of Paradise lost, that the absolute certainty that one man ruined us should give us an abounding guarantee that one glorious man has in very deed effectually saved all those who by faith accept the efficacy of his work.

Now, if you have grasped my thought, and have drunk into the truth of the text, you may derive a great deal of comfort from it, and it may suggest to you many painful things which will henceforth yield you pleasure. A babe is born into the world amid great anxiety because of its mother's pains, but while these go to prove how the consequences of the Fall are still with us, according to the word of the Lord to Eve, "in sorrow shalt thou bring forth children," they also assure us that the second Adam can abundantly bring us bliss through a second birth, by which we are begotten again unto a lively hope. You go into the arable field and mark the thistle, and tear your garments with a thorn: these prove the curse, but also preach the gospel. Did not the Lord God say, "Cursed is the ground for thy sake; thorns also and thistles shall it bring forth to thee." Through no fault of ours, for we were not present when the first man offended, our fields reluctantly yield their harvests. Well, inasmuch as we have seen the thorn and the thistle produced by the ground because of one Adam, we may expect to see a blessing on the earth because of the second and greater Adam. Therefore with unbounded confidence do I believe the promise—" Ye shall go out with joy, and be led forth with peace : the mountains and the hills shall break forth before you into singing, and all the trees of the field shall clap their hands. Instead of the thorn shall come up the fir tree, and instead of the brier shall come up the myrtle tree: and it shall be to the Lord for a name, for an everlasting sign that shall not be cut off."

Do you wipe the sweat from your brow as you toil for your livelihood? Did not the Lord say, "In the sweat of thy face shalt thou eat bread"? Ought not your labour to be an argument by which your faith shall prove that in Christ Jesus there remaineth a rest for the people of God. In toiling unto weariness you feel that Adam's fall is at work upon you; he has turned you into a tiller of the ground, or a keeper of sheep, or a worker in metals, but in any case he has made you wear a yoke; say you then to the Lord Jesus, "Blessed second Adam, as I see and feel what the first man did, I am abundantly certified as to what thou canst accomplish. I will therefore rest in thee with all my heart."

When you observe a funeral passing slowly along the street, or enter the churchyard, and notice hillock after hillock above the lowly beds of the departed, you see set forth evidently before your eyes the result of the Fall. You ask,—Who slew all these? and at what gate did the fell destroyer enter this world? Did the first Adam through his disobedience lift the latch for death? It is surely so. Therefore I believe with the greater assurance that the second Adam can give life to these dry bones, can awake all these sleepers, and raise them in newness of life. If so weak a man as Adam by one sin has brought in death, to pile the carcases of men heaps upon heaps, and make the earth reek with corruption, much more shall the glorious Son of God at his coming call them again to life and immortality, and renew them in the image of God. How blessed are those words,—"Now is Christ risen from the dead, and become the firstfruits of them that slept. For since by man came death, by man came also the resurrection of the dead. For as in Adam all die, even so in Christ shall all be made alive. The first man is of the earth, earthy: the second man is the Lord from heaven. As is the earthy, such are they also that are earthy : and as is the heavenly, such are they also that are heavenly. And as we have borne the image of the earthy, we shall also bear the image of the heavenly." Is not this killing a lion, and finding honey in its carcase? "Out of the eater cometh forth meat, and out of the strong cometh forth sweetness," when from the fact of the Fall we derive a strong assurance of our restoration by Christ Jesus.

Time fails me ; otherwise I meant to have dwelt somewhat at length upon the last head which can now only be cursorily noticed.

IV. It seems certain that if from the fall of Adam such great results flow, GREATER RESULTS MUST FLOW FROM THE GRACE OF GOD, AND THE GIFT BY GRACE, WHICH IS BY ONE MAN, JESUS CHRIST. Brethren, suppose that Adam had never sinned, and we were at this moment unfallen beings, yet our standing would have remained in jeopardy, seeing that at any moment he might have transgressed and so have pulled us down. Thousands of years of obedience might not have ended the probation, seeing there is no such stipulation in the original covenant. You and I therefore would be holding our happiness by a very precarious tenure ; we could never glory in absolute security and eternal life as we now do in Christ Jesus. We have now lost everything in Adam, and so the uncertain tenure has come to an end, our lease of Eden and its joys has altogether expired ; but we that have believed, have obtained an inheritance which we hold by an indisputable and never-failing title which Satan himself cannot dispute ; " All things are yours, and ye are Christ's, and Christ is God's." The Lord Jesus Christ has finished the work by which his people are saved, and that work has been certified by his resurrection from the dead. There are no " ifs " in the covenant now ; there is not a " peradventure " in it from beginning to end ; no chances of failure caused by unfinished conditions can be found in it. " He that believeth and is baptized *shall be saved.*" Do you say " I believe he shall be saved if he—"? Do not dare to add an " if " where God has placed none. Remember what will happen to you if you add anything to the book of God's testimony. No, it is written, " He that believeth and is baptized *shall be* saved :" " He that believeth in him hath *everlasting* life." " There is therefore now no condemnation to them that are in Christ Jesus." Thus we have obtained a surer standing than we could have had under the first Adam, and our hymn is true to the letter when it sings—

> " He raised me from the deeps of sin,
>   The gates of gaping hell,
>   And fix'd my standing more secure
>   Than 'twas before I fell."

Our Lord has not only undone the mischief of the Fall, but he has given us more than we have lost : even as the Psalmist saith, " Then I restored that which I took not away."

By the great transgression of Adam we lost our life in him, for so ran the threatening—" In the day that thou eatest thereof thou shalt surely die "; but in Christ Jesus we live again with a higher and nobler life, for the new life being the direct work of the Spirit, and being sustained by feeding upon the person of the Lord Jesus, is higher than the life of innocence in the garden of Eden. It is of a higher kind in many respects, of which we cannot now speak particularly, but this much we may say, " The first Adam was made a living soul, the second Adam is a quickening Spirit."

The Lord Jesus has also brought us into a nearer relationship to God than we could have possessed by any other means. We were God's creatures by creation, but now we are his sons by adoption ; in a certain narrow sense we were the offspring of God, but now by the exaltation of the man Christ Jesus, the representative of us all, we are brought into the nearest possible relationship to God. Jesus sits upon the throne of God, and manhood is thus uplifted next to deity : the nearest akin to the Eternal is a man, Christ Jesus, the Son of the Highest. We are members of his body, of his flesh, and of his bones, and therefore we share his honours and participate in his triumphs. In Christ Jesus man is made to have dominion over all the works of God's hands, and the redeemed are raised up together with Christ and made to sit in the heavenly places with him, above all principalities and powers, and all things else that be; for these are the favourites of heaven, the beloved of the great King. No creatures can equal perfected men; they rise superior even to the angels who have never sinned; for in them the riches of the glory of God's grace is more fully seen than in pure, unfallen spirits.

O beloved, hath not the Lord Jesus Christ done much for us, and ought we not to expect that it should be so, for the grace of God, and the gift by grace by the man Christ Jesus, are infinitely stronger forces than Adam's sin. There must be much more sap in the man, the Branch, than in that poor plant, the one man who was made from the dust of the earth. Oh the bliss which opens up before us now. We have lost Paradise, but we shall possess that of which the earthly garden was but a lowly type: we might have eaten of the luscious fruits of Eden, but now we eat of the bread which came down from heaven; we might have heard the voice of the Lord God walking in the garden in the cool of the day, but now, like Enoch, we may walk with God after a nobler and closer fashion. We are now capable of a joy which unfallen spirits could not have known: the bliss of pardoned sin, the heaven of deep conscious obligation to eternal mercy. The bonds which bind redeemed ones to their God are the strongest which exist. What a joy it will be to love the Lord more than any other of his creatures, and assuredly we shall do so. Do not think that this is an unwarrantable assertion, for I feel sure that it is the truth. Do you not read in the gospels of a woman who washed the Saviour's feet with tears and wiped them with the hairs of her head, and anointed them with ointment? Did not the Saviour say that she loved much because she had much forgiven. I take it that the same general principle will apply to all places, to eternity as well as to time, and therefore I believe that forgiven sinners will have a love to God and to his Christ such as cherubim and seraphim never felt; Gabriel cannot love Jesus as a forgiven man will do. Those who have washed their robes and made them white in the blood of the Lamb will be nearer and dearer to him, and he will be nearer and dearer to them, than all the ministering spirits before the throne, for he took upon him our nature and not theirs. Glory be unto thee, O Christ! As I look into the awful deeps of Adam's fall, I tremble, but when I lift up my eyes again to the eternal heights whither thou hast raised me by thy passion and thy resurrection I feel strengthened by the former vision. I magnify the infinite grace of God, and believe in it unstaggeringly. Oh, that I had power to magnify it with fit words and proper speech, but these are not with me. Accept the feeling of the heart when the language of the lip confesses its failure. Accept it, Lord, through the Well-beloved. Amen.

The Common Salvation

"The common salvation."—Jude 3.

JUDE says, " Beloved, when I gave all diligence to write unto you of the common salvation, it was needful for me to write unto you." The apostle did not write for writing's sake, and in this he sets us an example : we are not to speak for speaking's sake, nor even to preach for preaching's sake. When we take upon us to write concerning divine things it ought to be because it is needful for us to write, and when we speak in the name of God it should be because we have something to say which it is needful should be said. Unless a man feels an imperative necessity to speak he will not speak as an ambassador of God. I wot that Jude would not have given all diligence to write if he had not first felt that necessity was laid upon him so to do. Before you instruct others endeavour to feel the obligation which rests upon you to impart the light which you have received, for if you have been called of God unto this ministry woe is unto you if you preach not the gospel. The souls of others require the truth which you have been commissioned to teach; but you also require to teach it to them; for, if you do not warn them, their blood may stain your skirts. " That the soul be without knowledge is not good :" neither is it good to any that he should withhold what he knows. That men should live and die in ignorance of Christ is terrible to conceive of, therefore when you speak or write do it because it is needful to be done, and needful that you should do it. You know how it behoved Christ to suffer, and even so it behoves us to hold forth the word of life.

The necessity in the present case was that he should write of the common salvation. If it was common—commonly understood and commonly received—why should he need to write about it ? Surely a common subject has enough written upon it already, and it affords no room for freshness and novelty, which are so much desired by readers. Yet experience and observation prove that it is more needful to preach the common doctrines of the gospel than any other truths, and that just those things which appear to be the most elementary and the most generally received are those upon which it is most important to lay stress again and again. If there be certain high doctrines, speculative theories, and dogmas which are rather outgrowths of the gospel than the gospel itself, let them be preached in due proportion ; but if they be not preached, the risk and danger will not be extreme. As for the root facts, the fundamental doctrines, the primary truths of Scripture, we must from day to day insist upon them. We must never say of them, "Everybody knows them"; for, alas! everybody forgets them. We must not cease from proclaiming them from fear of being charged with uttering mere platitudes ; that which is revealed of the Holy Ghost must not be spoken of so reproachfully. Let men call the doctrines of the gospel platitudes if they will ; we will only answer, that on such platitudes our salvation rests. After all, on certain grand, wide, well-known truths of universal acceptance the church of God is builded; her basis is not a difficult philosophy, but a plain revelation. Let us not strain after matters of ultra refinement, theories of cultured intellects ; but let us obey the necessity which calls upon us to write and to speak of the common salvation. The gospel message is full of world-wide truisms and well-known facts. What said Paul,—"This is a faithful saying, and worthy of all acceptation, that Christ Jesus came into the world to save sinners." If worthy of all acceptation it is surely worthy of all proclamation. It is worth while for the whole church continually to rehearse that Jesus came to save sinners, for common truth as it is there is a necessity that we should perpetually and diligently make it known. The common salvation should be commonly spoken of ; but I fear it is uncommonly neglected in these days.

The immediate necessity to write of the common salvation arose out of certain men who had crept into the church unawares. Some of these attacked the gospel on its practical side with Antinomian subtlety. They cried up the grace of God, but said little of the holy living which it produces. They made light of sin under pretence of magnifying the grace of God ; they called careful watchfulness a legal spirit, derided humble self-examination, and claimed as children of God to be in no sense bound by the precepts of the moral law. The apostle calls it "turning the grace of our God into lasciviousness." Side by side with these there crept in another gang of evil ones, "who denied the only Lord God, and our Lord Jesus Christ." They robbed Christ of his divine glory, and so denied his atonement and sovereignty as to dethrone him from being either the Saviour or the King of his church. This was the essence of Arianism. They said that Jesus Christ was an admirable example, that he was one of a number of persons who have discovered important truths, and that he is therefore to be greatly admired; but they asserted that still higher truth would yet be discovered as the race proceeded in its progress, and so forth. These "men of thought" crept into the church, and stabbed at the heart of the common salvation. We used to have in our churches a sad amount of the Antinomian leaven ; we had among us men who preached the doctrine of grace without the grace of the doctrine, and professors who for evermore spoke about "the truth," but seemed little careful about following "the way" or exhibiting "the life." I hope that this evil principle has pretty well departed from us, though I fear that in its removal it has dragged away precious truth with it : and now we are assailed by quite another school of thought. I see no choice in the two kinds of foes, they are equally bad : these last are denying this truth and paring down the other, moving landmarks and overthrowing monuments, shaking every wall and kicking at every foundation. Having crept in among us unawares, defiant of common honesty, they preach against the gospel from our own pulpits and wage war against our Zion from within her own gates. It is essential at this day that such as fear God, and are his servants, should again and again both write and preach concerning "the common salvation," and over and over again rehearse the first lessons of Christ, the very alphabet of grace. We must make the joyful sound of the common salvation to be more common than ever. I wish to ring it out this morning with all the power that I have and with all that God will grant me by his Holy Spirit. If these men assailed certain speculations of theology it would little matter. What is the chaff to the wheat, saith the Lord? Let the chaff be removed, by all means. If they assailed certain peculiarities of method, either in work, or life, or teaching, it might be well for us to be taught something by their censures. If they attacked the specialities of a single person or sect, and the particular view of truth held by a mere party, it would not signify, for what are the fashions of men's minds? Who is Paul, and who is Apollos? But it is at the very root of the tree that they lay their axe, and, therefore, we must end all hesitation, take up our weapons, and for the sake of the common salvation earnestly contend for the faith which was once delivered unto the saints. Our subject, then, is "the common salvation." Oh to speak in the power of the Spirit.

I. Our first observation at this time shall be that PRESENT SALVATION IS ENJOYED BY THE FOLLOWERS OF CHRIST, otherwise there could be among them no "common salvation." Those who are sanctified by God the Father, and preserved in Jesus Christ, and called, are saved. In the church of God salvation is this day the privilege of all believers. *It is not a matter of the future alone,* a blessing to be sought for on a dying bed and reached in heaven; but it is a blessing for this world and this present time. Those greatly mistake the meaning of salvation who suppose it signifies nothing more than escaping from hell when you die and entering into heaven when the time has come. Salvation means being at once delivered from the power of sin, and being once for all washed from the guilt of sin. The very word used here—" the common salvation "—shows that Jude did not regard it as a hidden treasure put away from human reach throughout this mortal life. How could it have been common in such a case? He did not regard it as a distant attainment to be reached after twenty, thirty, or forty years of holy living, but as a thing to be tasted, and handled, and received as soon as faith enters the soul; for how else could it be common? " Unto us who are saved," says the apostle, " who hath saved us, and called us with an holy calling," saith the Scripture in another place. Salvation has come to our house, we have it, it is a common blessing in the household of faith.

As salvation is not a future benefit only, so *it is not a benefit reserved for a few of the more saintly people among believers.* It is supposed by some that you cannot know whether you are saved till you are in the article of death ; or that, if any do know it, it must be a few eminent teachers or specially holy persons, who have lived a very religious life, and consequently know that they are saved. It is to be confessed that the more holy and godly our life the brighter our evidence of salvation becomes; but still, the blessing itself is common to all the children of God, and those whose faith is feeble, and whose spiritual life is weak, are still saved in the Lord. Beloved hearer, you ought not to rest without knowing that you are saved. You may know it: if it be true you ought to know it. I do not think that you have any right to sit quietly on that seat for ten minutes without knowing that you are saved; for it is an awful thing to be in doubt as to whether you are under the bondage of sin, in doubt as to your being at peace with God. This is not a subject upon which uncertainty can be endured. You say, "'Tis a point I long to know." It is well that you long to know it: I beg you to long to know it so intensely that you must either know it or become unutterably wretched. Let every doubt on that point be like a sword in your bones. May God cause your heart either to rejoice with full assurance, or else to be in agony as with death pangs till you are confident that you are built on the sure foundation. The salvation which is in Christ Jesus is the common salvation of all who know the gospel and live upon it. Among simple-minded believers salvation is the inheritance of every one of them, and the knowledge that they are saved is an everyday possession. We who have joined in church-fellowship in this place can truly say, "We rejoice in Christ Jesus, and have no confidence in the flesh": "Being justified by faith, we have peace with God through our Lord Jesus Christ." We count it no presumption to say that we are saved, for the word of God has told us so in those places where salvation is promised to faith in Christ Jesus. The presumption would lie in doubting the word of God; but in simply believing what he says there is far greater humility than in questioning it. Being, then, partakers of like precious faith we share in salvation bought with precious blood, which though it be costly beyond all price is, nevertheless, to all believers the common salvation.

This common salvation consists in many works of grace for us and in us. In part it consists of deliverance from spiritual death. We were dead in trespasses and sins, but the Spirit of God has quickened us into a new and heavenly life, and thus we have salvation from spiritual death. This belongs to-day to all believers; for how can a man be a believer and not have the inner life? Having that life he is conscious that it is there. True, he may fall into a fainting fit, and lie swooning, scarcely conscious of being alive; but such is not his usual condition. Healthy life is conscious life, and rejoices in being, acting, and growing. You who are strangers to the people of God may think me fanatical, but, indeed, I am only speaking words of truth and soberness when I say that the conscious possession of a heavenly life is common among believers, and is, in fact, a large part of the common salvation.

This common salvation consists in deliverance from that awful distance at which we once stood from God. We were far off from him by wicked works, and when the quickening began in us we felt that distance, and we mourned it, fearing also that it never could be removed. But now in Christ Jesus we are brought nigh, and have become dwellers in the house of the Lord. Abba, Father, is the cry which the blessed God hears and accepts, as it rises from our hearts. Once God was not in all our thoughts, but now our thoughts are sanctified, and sweetened by a sense of his presence ; and we find our greatest joy in feeling that he is all around us and within us, that in him we live and move and have our being. Blessed is the common salvation which has brought us nigh to God by the blood of Jesus, and made us children and heirs of the Most High.

We have also been saved from the gloom of heart which once hung over us, because we were conscious of being under God's displeasure. We thought that we could never be forgiven, but we are forgiven; we concluded that our heavenly Father would never accept us, but we are accepted in the Beloved; we wrote ourselves down among the condemned, but now are we justified by faith which is in Christ Jesus our Lord. The darkness hath passed, and the true light shines into the spirits of the faithful. Peace with God is a sweet part of the common salvation.

Now are we delivered also from the love of sin. We cannot find pleasure in it as once we did. We sin, but it costs us dear. When we do so we lament it with our whole soul. It was our natural way to run the downward road, but now when our feet tread that path it is as wanderers who are out of their way. Once sin was our element, as the water is the living element of fish ; but it is far otherwise now, for sin is death to us. Transgression now breeds sorrow in our conscience, and creates misery in the heart, for it is alien to the life of God which is in us. If we could have our desire we would never offend again : we would have our souls clear as the firmament above us, and never should an evil thought or a loose desire flit over the pure heavens of our sanctified minds. We would do God's will on earth as it is done in heaven ; I say "we," for I speak for all believers in the Lord Jesus. We are all rescued from the iron yoke of the love of evil, and this is a most precious part of the common salvation.

The Lord has also delivered us from that cowardly fear of man which bringeth a snare, and holdeth men as slaves to evil customs. He has also brought us out of the dark dungeon of spiritual ignorance, and renewed us in knowledge ; thus has he broken the dominion of the former lusts of our ignorance, and given us liberty to serve him with godly fear. Pride, too, is laid in the dust, and we are saved from that dreadful tyrant. The dominant power of selfishness is destroyed, and we have learned to love. The woes of others afflict us, the joys of others rejoice us, our soul flows out beyond the narrow confines of our own ribs. Our heart is enlarged with love towards God and to all his creatures. Blessed salvation this ! And it is common to all believers.

We have again and again heard it said that evangelical ministers preach salvation to sinful men and talk to them of a future life, whereas if we were practical we should denounce the sinner, and speak only of present reformation in this life. The charge is, I fear, oftener made in malice than in ignorance. But if in ignorance I would reply,—O fools and slow of heart, neither to hearken nor to understand. Our constant theme is immediate salvation from sin, and we are perpetually insisting upon it that this salvation is a present business, to be attended to at once for the purposes of to-day. It is false, utterly false, that we have so preached about the world to come as to have pushed out of sight the duties and temptations of this present life. No, we have regarded the life to come as commenced here below, and have viewed heaven itself as to a great extent the fruit of a heavenly disposition which must be implanted in us while yet on earth. Ah, if men did not hate the gospel they would not so often repeat stale objections and groundless accusations. It is surely time that infidelity should invent something fresh in the way of objection, for this has long passed the stage of toleration, and has become a worn-out impertinence.

Salvation from sin, leading upward to perfection and heaven, is called in the text "the common salvation." It is, then, the salvation of all God's people—the salvation about which all true Christians are agreed; for, notwithstanding all you hear about our divisions into sects, the church is really one. The denominations of the Christian church are very like the divisions of a ploughed field by means of furrows which mark the surface, but the land remains to all intents and purposes one field. I speak not of mere professors, but truly spiritual people; such are all one in Christ Jesus, and their salvation is in all respects the same. If they have not all things common, at least they have one and the same salvation. All converted men and women believe in the same essential truths, feel the working of the same Spirit within them, and press forward to the same end, namely, perfecting holiness in the fear of the Lord. You shall take a high churchman, who is a truly spiritual man, and there are such people, and you shall set him down side by side with the most rigid member of the Society of Friends, and when they begin to talk of Jesus, of the work of the Holy Spirit in the soul, and the desire of their hearts after God, you will hardly know which is which. The nearer we come to him who is the salvation of God, the more plainly we see that among the children of God the basis of agreement is far wider than the ground of division. Andrew Fuller well and pithily said, " There are, I conceive, four things which essentially belong to the common salvation ; its necessity, its vicarious medium, its freeness to the chief of sinners, and its holy efficacy." We may differ on the " five points," but we are agreed upon these four points. Ask any true Christian if it be not so. You shall get together, if you like, a collection of the odds and ends of Christianity—and certainly there are some queer Christian people about, whose light comes from above, so they say,—I think through a crack in the roof; but if they are really genuine, and their hearts are right, you shall find that even in these wrong-headed folk there is an agreement upon their need of a Saviour, their faith in his death, the freeness of his grace, and the change of heart which it produces. All believers in Christ have a common delight in a common salvation.

II. We go a step further, and note, secondly, that THIS SALVATION IS IN SOME RESPECTS COMMON IN THE WIDEST POSSIBLE SENSE. It is common because *it is to be preached to all nations,* to all classes, to all characters, to all ages, and to all conditions of men—in fact, it is to be preached to every creature under heaven. It is the common salvation so far as this, that a proclamation of mercy through Jesus Christ is to be made to all mankind ; for it is declared that if they believe in Christ Jesus they shall be saved. You need not be afraid of being too free and unreserved in your delivering of the gospel. Let the great trumpet be blown, and let every mortal ear attend. I am as firm an adherent to the doctrines of sovereign grace as any man living ; but never shall this tongue hesitate to declare the common salvation. Whenever I am called upon to address a congregation, I will always cry, " Ho, every one that thirsteth, come ye to the waters !" " Whosoever will, let him take of the water of life freely." The invitation of the gospel is so far-reaching that it may well be called " the common salvation."

It is common in the widest sense, because *every man that believeth in Christ Jesus will be saved* ; not the Jew only, but the Gentile also ; not the poor man only, but the rich man also ; not the black man only, or the white man only, but men of every colour ; not the ignorant or the learned, the rude or the refined, exclusively, but every soul of Adam born that believeth in Christ Jesus shall be saved. " For God so loved the world that he gave his only begotten Son, that whosoever believeth in him should not perish, but have everlasting life." And so to thee, dear hearer, whoever thou mayest be, comes this common salvation. It is a command addressed to thee, and a promise made sure to thee : " Believe in the Lord Jesus Christ, and thou shalt be saved."

It is common in this wide sense, that *if any man be saved he will be saved by this common salvation.* Men talk as if there were half-a-dozen different roads to heaven, and yet there is but one : they prattle as if there were seven or eight Saviours at the least, or as if every man must be his own Saviour, as we heard the other day of every man being his own lawyer ; and yet there is but one name given among men whereby we must be saved. He who tries to be his own Saviour has a fool for his client. He will utterly fail to his eternal confusion : why did Jesus die to save us if we can save ourselves? All of Adam born who enter eternal life come in by the one door. Infants are saved through Christ, and if any attain to heaven from among the heathen it must be by virtue of the salvation of Christ. He is the common life for all that live, the common bread for all who are fed by God, the common joy of all who have been blessed of the Lord. Thus in its publication, in its promise, and in its efficacy the salvation of Christ is the one and only gospel of life to men. As there is but one common air, one common sea, one common earth, so there is but one common salvation. O that we may be among those who prove its power in their own person by being saved in the Lord with an everlasting salvation.

III. But I am persuaded that this is not what Jude meant, so I come, in the third place, to say that IT IS COMMON TO ALL BELIEVERS. Do you recollect what this same Jude once said to the Saviour? He asked him, " Lord, how is it that thou wilt manifest thyself unto us and not unto the world?" He understands that matter now ; but he is not looking so much at the "not unto the world" as at the first fact in his question, "Thou wilt manifest thyself unto us." He is evidently full of joy that the manifestation of the salvation of Jesus is common to all believers. Upon that blessed fact let us dwell.

Certain offices, gifts, attainments and enjoyments are given to some and not to others. "Are all apostles? are all prophets? are all teachers? are all workers of miracles? Have all the gifts of healing? do all speak with tongues? do all interpret?" It is not every believer that possesses full assurance, or enjoys ecstasy, or is made largely useful to others. But all believers have the common salvation. There they share and share alike, and every one of them is saved in Christ Jesus and called. An apostle may say to the newest of his converts, " I long to see you, that I may impart unto you some spiritual gift, to the end ye may be established; that is, that I may be comforted together with you by the mutual faith both of you and me."

For, first, it is a common salvation which all believers possess, since it springs from *the same grace.* There are not some saved by grace and others by works, many by pure grace and more partly by works; but salvation is altogether of grace in every case, and that grace is the same in all who possess it. All believers are chosen by the same electing love, for the same reason, namely, to the glory of the Father's grace; and being so chosen, they are all ordained unto the same life, secured by the same covenant, and given into the hands of the same Surety. Eternal love encompasses, enriches, comforts, and preserves each individual believer, and guarantees to each the same inheritance in Christ Jesus. Brother, are you saved by grace ? so am I. Am I saved by grace ? Then my sister, if thou believest in Christ, thou art saved as I am.

It is a common salvation—common because we are all saved by *the same Saviour.* We are not some of us looking to Jesus, and others to Moses, or to ourselves ; neither are we some of us looking to the atoning death, and others to the perfect life of Christ ; but we are all saved by the same one work, life, death, resurrection and intercession of Christ Jesus. When he made atonement by blood it was for all his redeemed ; when he rose it was to justify all who are in him ; when he stands at the right hand of God to plead, he intercedes for all the saints ; and when he cometh it will be that all his saints may be with him where he is, and may behold his glory. Do not fall into the modern notion, which divides up Christ, and allots something to one class of believers, and another portion to others of the chosen. They tell us there are such and such promises for Israel, and other promises for the church ; I have not so read the word, for I am persuaded that all believers are the Israel of God. God loveth all his saints, and the same blessedness shall be to them all, and you may rejoice and be glad that God will not give special raptures and upsoarings into the skies to a portion of his family, and leave the rest in the cold. In all that is "salvation" we have a common heritage, for Christ belongs to us all, and we are all members of his body, partakers of his life, and sharers of his glory.

It is a common salvation because we are all saved through the *same faith,* we believe the same precious truth, and receive Christ in the same way. All the saved possess faith, though not all to the same degree. Would God we were all strong in faith ! Still, faith is a child-like confidence in God in the greatest as much as in the least of God's people, and this is the essential requisite to salvation in every case. He that believeth in Christ is not condemned, but he that believeth not is condemned already. To all participation in Christian privilege we have only one right : " If thou believest with all thy heart thou mayest." Faith makes a man a fellow-commoner with the saints of God.

It is a common salvation because faith and spiritual life are wrought in us by the *same Spirit.* Faith does not come to one by the operation of free will and to another by free grace, but to every one by the same Spirit. You, then, my brother, are plucked like a brand from the burning by the power of the Spirit of God, so also is thy friend who rejoices with thee. All are quickened by the same Spirit, and kept alive by the same Quickener. The love of the Spirit should be joyfully acknowledged by us all without exception, for the Spirit has wrought all our works in us.

It is a common salvation as to *its results ;* for all believers are equally born again, and they are all renewed by him, who saith, "Behold I make all things new." Brought into the one family of God, they are all made children of God and joint heirs with Christ Jesus. They are all justified, accepted, preserved, guided, upheld, and comforted. Their feet are set upon the selfsame rock, they are led in the same King's highway, and a new song is prepared for every one of their mouths. The common salvation, like the common table of a household, satisfies all their mouths with good things, and renews their youth like the eagle's.

By-and-by they shall meet in *the same heaven.* There will be no division before the throne between the different tribes and denominations of believers. One family, we dwell in him even now, with all our petty strifes ; but the great family relationship shall be more fully developed by-and-by when imperfections and errors shall be cast aside. The saints before the throne will sing a common hymn unto the common Saviour as they gather in the common home, saved with a common salvation.

Brethren, I am right glad of all this. I feel inclined to stop the sermon and ask you to join in singing Charles Wesley's verse—

> " Partners of a glorious hope,
> Lift your hearts and voices up ;
> Jointly let us rise and sing
> Christ our Prophet, Priest, and King."

To me it is a joyous thing that God's best gifts should be the commonest. It is so in nature : the sunshine, the dew, the air, the heavens, these cannot become the particular estate of a few ; they are common blessings. When Richard the Second banished Bolingbroke that nobleman is represented as saying—

> " This must my comfort be,
> That sun that warms you here, shall shine on me ;
> And those his golden beams, to you here lent,
> Shall point on me, and gild my banishment."

There is no monopolizing the best gifts, for heaven ordains them to be the right of all mankind ; and so the chief things of the covenant of grace are common to all believers. One may have greater powers of speech than another ; but God hath spoken to the silent brother the same promises. Gifts are to this man and to that ; but the gift of salvation is to all who believe. The choicest saint may have far less of this world's riches than his brother ; but the riches of God's grace are all his own by equal title. We live on common ground here, fed by our Father with the same bread from heaven. Thank God that in so many points the saints have fellowship, for all these should make them of one mind and of one heart towards each other. Some of God's children are not learned, but they shall all be taught of the Lord ; all are not experienced in the deep things of God, but they are all entitled to the best things of God. There are some few points in which we are unlike, even as children of the same family differ in age, and height, or in the colour of their eyes or hair ; but we are one in so many vital and conspicuous features, that we should with one voice and heart praise our common Father. We may not all wear the same form of garment, but we all breathe the same life. We may not eat from the same ware, but we all eat the same bread. We may not all drink from a silver chalice, but the wine is from the one cluster. "Now there are diversities of gifts, but the same Spirit. And there are differences of administrations, but the same Lord. And there are diversities of operations, but it is the same God which worketh all in all" It is a great comfort to my heart that, among you who are bound to me by such loving ties, I can speak without hesitation of the common salvation ; for you know it, feel it, love it, rejoice in it, even as I do this day.

IV. That brings me to close, by noticing that this fact of the common salvation was mentioned by Jude that he might use it as an argument. So then THIS FACT HAS MANY LESSONS IN IT.

First, this common salvation *forbids a monopolizing spirit.* The old divines used to say that enclosures were contrary to law. I am afraid that I may not say so now; for almost everywhere the commons have been taken from the poor man and his goose. May there yet be an end to such enclosings. But enclosures in spiritual things are contrary to the law of Christ. Who are we that we should cut off from fellowship with us those whose fellowship is with the Father and his Son Jesus Christ? Yet we have those around us who make it a point of Christianity to be *exclusive.* Their exclusions are perpetual. Shut that door ! Shut that door ! Shut that door ! seems to be the one great command of their house, and the second is like unto it—make more doors, one within the other, and take care to bolt them all. Their sheep must keep within their fold without fail, for if they once get a bite of pasture outside the enclosure their doom is sealed. In many forms this spirit has has been among our denominations, but I do not believe in it. If the spirit of Christianity begets in us love to all mankind, much more, my brethren, are we to love those in whom there is the life of God. Is it really so, that this man is to be un-Christianized because of a mistake and the other because of a misapprehension? Doth God make thy brother a Christian and dost thou try to unmake him? Doth God think so much of him as to forgive him, to give him power in prayer, and enjoyment of his presence, and dost thou think so lightly of him that thou wilt hardly own him to be a partaker in Christ at all? Does the Father smile on all his children, and do we frown on half of them? If I could do it, the last thing I should attempt would be to wall in my own special company and say, "The temple of the Lord are we." I would not wish to set a fence round about the baptized and say, "These be the church of Christ, even as many as have been immersed in water that they may be buried into his death." Beloved brethren, our Lord hath a people that are on other points as right as right can be who on the point of baptism are as wrong as wrong can be; but, for all that, they are his people, and in other respects are sound in the faith and valiant for the Lord our God. Unto such our love goeth forth, and must go forth, despite their grievous error. Upon other matters there are distinctions among believers, but yet there is a common salvation enjoyed by the Arminian as well as by the Calvinist, possessed by the Presbyterian as well as by the Episcopalian, prized by the Quaker as well as by the Baptist. Those who are in Christ are more near of kin than they know of, and their intense unity in deep essential truth is a greater force than most of them imagine : only give it scope and it will work wonders. As for us, let us not be among the men of whom Jude says, "These be they that separate themselves, sensual, having not the Spirit."

Next, this doctrine *fosters the spirit of benediction.* Jude begins his epistle with "Mercy unto you, and peace, and love be multiplied." Brothers and sisters, fill your lungs with this healthy air. You are saved with a common salvation ; desire the profit, the growth, the happiness of all who partake of this one salvation. You are in one ship ; seek the good of all who sail with you. You are enlisted in one army ; pray the Captain of salvation to make every soldier strong in the Lord and in the power of his might. The common salvation should excite us to seek the prosperity of every part of Zion ; we would seek the good, not of our Tabernacle alone, but of every tabernacle or temple where Christians meet to worship the Most High.

Next, this fact *arouses in us a common spirit of contention for the one faith.* For what saith the apostle ? "It is needful that I write unto you of the common salvation, and exhort you that you should earnestly contend for the faith once delivered to the saints." When the gospel is assailed we must all rise in its defence, for it is the common salvation which is involved in it. When they frightened this nation years ago with the rumour of an invasion by the French, the Russians, or somebody or other, what was the result ? Everybody became warlike. Our young men joined rifle clubs, and our elderly men furbished up their old blunderbusses. Everybody hastened to arm himself to protect the common country from the coming foe ; and had the enemy really arrived even the women would have shouldered their brooms to sweep the intruder over our white cliffs. Every man, woman, and child would have found some fork, or scythe, or spade, or axe wherewith to protect the common fatherland. Community of interest begets community of feeling. We are all Englishmen, and we all sing, "Britons never will be slaves" ; so, in this case, when the gospel of Jesus Christ is assailed, it does not matter by whom, I feel I may call upon all Christians to take action for the common salvation. Brothers, rouse you to the fight, for more than our hearths and homes is now attacked. Do they deny the deity of Christ ? It is not only *my* religion that is assailed, it is yours as well. Do they turn the grace of God into lasciviousness ? It is not this branch of the church that is now endangered. The entire church is placed in jeopardy. This gospel is not my heritage or yours, it is the common domain of all the faithful, and I beseech you feel it to be so. In your own spheres and in your own ways hold the truth, and hold it firmly. You who can neither preach nor write in defence of sound doctrine can at least give negative help by refusing to countenance error. Do not go to hear those who preach false doctrine, do not encourage them in any way, do not bid them God speed. Love all them that love the Lord Jesus Christ in sincerity, but if a word be spoken against the Lord or against the gospel which he has revealed, turn your back upon the speaker. Be like the loving John, who, when he went to take a bath, found Cerinthus, the heretic, there, and departed at once with all speed. I want to see more backbone in all professors, more determination never to stultify their faith by pretending to believe that black is white and that white is a shade of black. Love: do I not preach it with all my heart, and do I not bid you manifest it in your deeds? But with that love mingle a firm adherence to the truth as it is in Jesus, and a zealous resolve that it shall not lose its honour while you are capable of upholding it. Let the common salvation be protected by the earnest zeal of the entire body of the church and by us also.

This fact, I think, *puts everyone of us to the question*, It is a common salvation, but have I a part in it? It belongs to all the people of God, but am I one of them? I should like you this morning, when you get home, to write on a piece of paper, if you will, whether you are saved or not. It would be a timely searching. Here you are, on this tenth of April—write down " Saved, bless the Lord for it," and if you are obliged to feel you could not write that down, go up into your chamber and cry mightily unto God till you can. Well, if you are able to write " saved," then inasmuch as it is a common salvation go and try to spread that salvation among others. " Others save," says Jude. I know, he says, " others save with fear," but still he says " others save ; " try as far as ever you can to bring others to the Saviour. A man's salvation that he never wishes to spread among others is a salvation that is not worth having. You are not saved from selfishness if you do not wish to see your children, and relatives, and neighbours, yea, and all the world brought to Jesus' feet. If it be a common salvation go and make it common.

And, lastly, this text *calls for a common song of praise* from all those who have the common salvation, and I cannot suggest to you a better doxology than that with which Jude closes his epistle : " Now unto him that is able to keep you from falling, and to present you faultless before the presence of his glory with exceeding joy, to the only wise God our Saviour, be glory and majesty, dominion and power, both now and ever. Amen."

One More Cast of the Great Net

"And it shall come to pass, that whosoever shall call on the name of the Lord shall be delivered: for in mount Zion and in Jerusalem shall be deliverance, as the Lord hath said, and in the remnant whom the Lord shall call."—Joel ii. 32.

I THOUGHT within myself, "What shall be the topic for the last sermon before I depart to my quiet resting-place?" Peradventure my sermons for the last day of this long stretch of work may be my last altogether, for life is very frail. When I hear of first one and then another in strong health being suddenly taken away, I am made to know the uncertainty of life in my own case. It were wiser to trust a spider's cobweb than the life of man. Brethren, we live on the brink of eternity, and had need behave ourselves as men who will soon face its realities. We may have to do so far sooner than we think. So I said within myself, "Shall I feed the flock of God in the rich pastures of choice promise?" Truly it would have been well to have done so; but then I bethought me of the stray sheep; must I not go after *them?* The ninety and nine are not in the wilderness, and, therefore, I shall not be leaving them in any danger. They are well folded, and the Chief Shepherd will not forget them. God has given them to have life in themselves, and the green pastures are with them in plenty; they can afford to be let alone better than the perishing ones. But as for the wandering ones, can I leave them among the wilds and wolves? I have tried to bring them to the great Bishop and Shepherd of souls, but they have not yet returned; how can I forget them? How can I endure to think of their being lost for ever?

So I thought I would go out once more after the lost ones hoping that the Lord would help me to find them, even now, and bring them to himself! I earnestly ask your prayers that a very simple gospel address may be blessed of God to the immediate conversion of those among us who have long halted, and are hesitating even unto this day. I could not have chosen for such a purpose a more suitable text: it is one of the broadest declarations of gospel doctrine that could be found in Holy Scripture.

I shall handle it in the plainest manner. In a book of practical surgery you do not look for figures of speech; all is plain as a pike-staff; such will my sermon be. I hand out the bread of heaven, and you do not expect poetry from a bakehouse.

When the apostle Peter was preaching what I may call the inauguration sermon of the evangelical era, he could do no better than go to Joel for his text. See the second chapter of the Acts of the Apostles. He explained the wonders of the Pentecost by a reference to this prophetic passage. When Paul, in his famous Epistle to the Romans, would set out the gospel in all its plainness, he could not do better than quote in his tenth chapter, at the thirteenth verse, this same text : " For whosoever shall call upon the name of the Lord shall be saved." If apostles found this passage so suitable for the expression and confirmation of their gospel message, what can I do but follow their wise example ? How greatly do I hope that a blessing will rest upon all here present while I preach upon this precious portion of Scripture ; even as a blessing rested upon the motley crowd in Jerusalem when Peter spoke to them ! The same Spirit is with us, and his sacred power is not in the least diminished. Why should he not convert three thousand now, as he did on that occasion ? If there be a failure, it will not arise from him, but from ourselves.

Look at the connection of our text in Joel, and you will find that it is preceded by terrible warnings: " I will shew wonders in the heavens and in the earth, blood, and fire, and pillars of smoke. The sun shall be turned into darkness, and the moon into blood, before the great and the terrible day of the Lord come." Nor is this all; this broad gospel statement is followed by words of equal dread. "Let the heathen be wakened, and come up to the valley of Jehoshaphat: for there will I sit to judge all the heathen round about. Put ye in the sickle, for the harvest is ripe : come, get you down ; for the press is full, the fats overflow ; for their wickedness is great. The sun and the moon shall be darkened, and the stars shall withdraw their shining." It was true of the prophets as of the apostles that, knowing the terrors of the Lord, they persuaded men. They were not ashamed to use fear as a powerful motive with mankind. By the prophet Joel the diamond of our text is placed in a black setting, and its brilliance is thereby enhanced. As a lamp is all the more valued when the night is dark, so is the gospel all the more precious when men see their misery without it. To remove from men's minds the salutary fear of punishment for sin is to draw up the flood-gates of iniquity. He who does this is a traitor to society. If men are not warned of the anger of God against iniquity, they will take license to riot in evil.

Certain modern teachers pretend that they are so delicate that, if they believed in the Scriptural doctrine of eternal punishment, they could never smile again. Poor sufferers ! One is therefore led to suppose that they are persons of superior piety, who are so deeply in love with the souls of men that they weep over them day and night, and labour to bring them to repentance. We should expect to see in them a perpetual agony for the good of their fellows, since they judge themselves to be so qualified to instruct others in the art of compassion. But, my brethren, we have not been able to discover in these sensitive persons any very hallowed sympathy with the ungodly ; nay, we have heard of their having communion with the worldly in their sports rather than in their sorrow for sin. I have not seen in these men who forswear the use of the terrors of the Lord any remarkable powers of attracting men to Jesus by love. I have not noted any special zeal in them for the conversion of men, either by tender arguments, or by any other means. I question if they believe in conversion at all. On the other hand, the seraphic evangelists who have journeyed around the earth to preach the gospel, and have worn themselves down with evangelical earnestness, are, in all cases, men who feel the pressure of the wrath to come. These, though sneered at by the superfine delicates, have shown a tender love to which their judges are strangers.

He who speaks honestly concerning the judgment to come is the man of the tenderest heart. He who pleads with sinners, even to tears, usually does so because he believes that they will be everlastingly ruined except they repent. I do not believe that this modern zeal to conceal the justice of God and hide the punishment of sin is accompanied by an overflowing compassion for souls; I fear that, on the contrary, it is little other than an incidental form of a flippant unbelief which treats all doctrines of God's Word as antiquated notions, deserving to be jested at by men of advanced views. My brethren, the love of Jesus did not prevent his warning men of future woe. He cried aloud, amid a flood of tears, " O Jerusalem, Jerusalem, how often would I have gathered thy children together ! " and he did not withhold the dreadful fact— " Your house is left unto you desolate." The knowledge of the coming destruction of the city aroused his sympathy; and he showed his pity, not by concealing the dreadful future, but by warning men of it. I venture to say that, so far as I have observed, no man ever preaches the gospel at all unless he has a deep and solemn conviction that sin will be punished in a future state in a manner most just and terrible. Preachers gradually get further and further away from the gospel, and its atoning sacrifice, in proportion as they delude themselves with the idea that, after all, sin is a small matter, and its punishment a questionable severity. Those also who look for a future opportunity for the impenitent may well consider it to be of small consequence whether men now believe in Jesus, or remain in unbelief. Such a taking of things easy cannot suggest itself to me, for I believe in everlasting punishment. O my hearers, if you do not fly to Jesus, you will be eternally lost, and this urges me to entreat you to be saved! That blood and fire, that darkening sun and crimsoned moon, of which Joel speaks, arouse me to exhort you to seek deliverance. That great white throne, and the dread sentence of him that shall sit upon it, when he shall say, " Depart from me, ye cursed, into everlasting fire, prepared for the devil and his angels," all move me to persuade you to flee to Jesus. Therefore it is my delight to come to you with a free, broad, blessed, gospel promise, in the earnest hope that those of you who are now in danger may at once escape for your lives, and flee from the wrath to come.

With that preface I come to the handling of my text, moved by a burning desire that God may bless it. First notice that it contains *a glorious proclamation*—" It shall come to pass, that whosoever shall call on the name of the Lord shall be delivered." But this is accompanied with an *instructive declaration*, to which we shall give a measure of attention as time permits—" In mount Zion and in Jerusalem shall be deliverance, as the Lord hath said, and in the remnant whom the Lord shall call."

I. Listen, first, to THE GLORIOUS PROCLAMATION. As we have no time to spare, we will proceed at once to our theme.

The blessing proclaimed in our text is precious.—" Whosoever shall call on the name of the Lord shall be delivered," or " shall be *saved.*" Salvation is a very comprehensive blessing; it is, in fact, a constellation of favours: a mass of mercies condensed into a word. It is a boon which reaches from the door of hell to the gate of heaven. The salvation which we have to preach to you at this time is salvation from sin in all senses of that term. It is a diamond with many facets. You who dread the eternal consequences of iniquity will be glad to learn that there is salvation from the punishment of sin—complete and eternal salvation. This is no small matter to a soul crushed beneath a consciousness of guilt, and the certainty that the necessary consequences of sin must be overwhelming. The results of sin are not to be thought of without trembling. Verily, dismay may well take hold of the stoutest heart while reflecting upon the judgment to come. We preach salvation from the unutterable woe which follows on the heels of sin. Whatever may be the terrors of that tremendous day, for which all other days were made, we proclaim in God's name salvation from them all. Whatever may be the gloom of that bottomless abyss, into which the guilty shall sink for ever, we are enabled to proclaim complete deliverance from that endless fall—salvation for every soul that believeth in Jesus Christ the Lord. No form of accusation shall be drawn up against the believer. No sentence of condemnation shall ever be uttered against him. Salvation sends the prisoner out of court completely cleared. All the penal consequences of all sin shall be turned aside from all who by divine grace are led to call upon the name of the Lord.

Salvation also delivers from the guilt of sin. The Lord is able to justify the ungodly so that he shall be numbered with the righteous. Through the blood of Jesus he makes the filthy whiter than the snow. He will not merely put away the sin itself, but all the defilement that has come of it to your moral manhood. O my hearer, all the injury which you have already inflicted upon yourself by sin, the Lord can repair! Sin, even if it led to no penal consequences, is a disease which destroys the beauty of your manhood, and makes us loathsome to the eye of God—ay, and shocking to the view of our own conscience, when we see ourselves by the light of God's Spirit in the glass of his Word. O ye, on whose foreheads the leprosy is white, we preach perfect healing for you, a salvation which shall renovate your nature, and make your flesh even as the flesh of a little child; as Naaman's was when he came up from the washing, having been obedient to the prophetic command. Brethren, the salvation of the Lord removes every injurious result of sin upon heart and mind. Is not this a joy ?

We also preach salvation from the power of sin. Sin finds a nest in the carnal nature, but it hides there as a thief ; it shall not have dominion over you, for ye are not under law, but under grace. O slaves, whose fetters clank in your ears, at this moment you may be free! Whether the bonds be those of drunkenness, or licentiousness, or worldliness, or despair, the Lord looseth the prisoners. Jesus has come to break the manacles from your wrists, the fetters from your feet. If the Son shall make you free, you shall be free indeed. He has come to set you free for holiness, for purity, for peace, for love. He will bless you with newness of life: he will cause grace to reign in you unto eternal life. Salvation from the power of evil is a gift worthy of a God. This is the salvation that we preach: we proclaim immediate deliverance from the curse of sin, present rescue from the power of sin, and ultimate freedom from the very being of sin. To every man of woman born is this salvation proclaimed, provided they will obey the gospel command, which saith—look unto Christ, and live. "Whosoever shall call on the name of the Lord shall be saved." Happy herald who has such a proclamation to make! The boon is incalculably precious.

Further, notice, in the next place, that *the time of this proclamation is present;* for Peter tells us that the time spoken of by the prophet Joel began at Pentecost. When the rushing, mighty wind was heard, and the flaming tongues sat upon the disciples' heads, then was the gospel dispensation opened in all its freeness. The Holy Ghost, who then came down to earth, has never returned; he is still in the midst of the church, not working physical wonders, but performing moral and spiritual miracles in our midst, even to this day. To-day, through his power, full remission is preached to every repenting sinner; to-day is complete salvation promised to every one that believeth in Jesus. This day the promise stands true, "Whosoever shall call on the name of the Lord shall be saved."

I put aside as altogether unscriptural the notion that the day of grace is past for any man who will call upon the name of the Lord. If you will call, you shall be heard, be the day what it may; yea, though it wane to the eleventh hour. The day of grace is never past to any soul that lives, as long as it is willing to believe in Jesus. I am not told to go and say there is grace for men up to a certain point, and beyond that point there is none. No, there is no limit set to the willingness or ability of Christ to save those who call upon his name. Who dares to limit the Holy One of Israel in the deeds of his grace? As long as faith is possible, salvation is possible. I have my Master's order to preach the gospel to every creature. He has said to his servants, "As many as ye shall find, bid to the marriage." We are bound to say to every one, "He that believeth and is baptized shall be saved; but he that believeth not shall be damned." Whether you are a child of ten, or a man of fifty, I have the same message for you. If you have lived to be a hundred, the gospel promise still holds good, despite the lapse of years. The times of your ignorance God has winked at; but he now commandeth all men everywhere to repent. He graciously declares of all who seek him, "Him that cometh to me I will in no wise cast out." Day of grace past, indeed! It is a whisper of Satan. Have nothing to do with that falsehood; for still the Saviour bids you come to him and live. Even at the ebb of life he cries, "Come now, and let us reason together."

> "Life is the time to seek his face
> Through life he freely gives his grace,
> And while that lamp holds out to burn,
> The vilest sinner may return."

Whoever returns to the Father's house shall find a glad reception. If this very day, this 14th of November, you will call upon the Lord, you shall be saved. God speaks by my mouth to you at this moment, and declares that to-day, if *you* will hear his voice, *your* soul shall live. The proverb saith, "there is no time like time present," and it speaks the truth. The present moment is the best moment in your possession. What other moment have you? Whosoever, at this passing hour, calleth upon the name of the Lord shall be saved. This is a gospel well worth the preaching: blessed are our ears that we hear the joyful sound!

Next, notice that, as the boon is precious, and the time is present, so *the range of this proclamation is promising.* It is full of good cheer to all who hear me this day. " *Whosoever* shall call on the name of the Lord shall be saved." *Whosoever!* I am afraid lest anything I should say to express the width of this word should only narrow it; just as the man who tries to explain eternity always makes it seem much shorter than we thought it to be, and so defeats his own purpose. " *Whosoever.*" There is in this word no fence, or ditch, or boundary line. You are out upon the open mountains of grace. In riding through Switzerland you will find gates put up here and there along the road, for no reason that I could see but to tax and worry travellers: many of the limits which are set to the gospel proclamation answer no other purpose. Down with these toll-bars on the road to heaven! We cannot and dare not discourage any man from calling on the name of the Lord : the promise is to you, and to your children; but it is also to all "that are afar off, even as many as the Lord our God shall call." In this matter there is no difference between Jew and Gentile. "Whosoever" includes the slum people, even the poorest of the poor; but it does not exclude the carriage people, not even the richest of the rich. "Whosoever" beckons to the educated, and looks favourably upon the cultured and the refined : but none the less does it invite the illiterate, to whom all learning is an unattainable mystery. "Whosoever" has a finger for babes, and an arm for old men; it has an eye for the quick, and a smile for the dull.

Young men and maidens, *whosoever* offers its embrace to you! Good and bad, honourable or disreputable, this "whosoever" speaks to you all with equal truth! Kings and queens may find room in it; and so may thieves and beggars. Peers and paupers sit on one seat in this word. "Whosoever" has a special voice *for you,* my hearer! Do you answer, "But I am an oddity"? "Whosoever" includes all the oddities. I always have a warm side towards odd, eccentric, out-of-the-way people, because I am one myself, at least so I am often said to be. I am deeply thankful for this blessed text; for if I am a lot unmentioned in any other catalogue, I know that this includes me : I am beyond all question under the shade of "whosoever." No end of odd people come to the Tabernacle, or read my sermons; but they are all within the range of "whosoever."

"Alas!" cries one, "I am dreadfully desponding, I am too low-spirited to be intended by the promise of grace!" Are you? I do not believe it. "Whosoever" goes to the very depths of despair, and up to the heights of glory. "Alas!" murmurs another, "I am not sad enough on account of my sin. I am of too frivolous a nature!" Very likely, but "whosoever" includes *you;* if *you* call on the Lord, *you* shall be saved. You may go round the whole Tabernacle this morning, and "whosoever" will include all the thousands in it : after that you may hasten down the streets, and tramp from end to end of London's mighty area, and never find one left out. You may then take a tourist's ticket, and travel through Europe, Africa, and Asia, till you have even traversed China and Japan. You may sweep the southern seas, and search Australia, and then come home by way of San Francisco, and in all that circular tour you will not have met man, woman, or child, whether white, or black, or red, or yellow, or blue, or green, but what is encompassed by the circle of this word "whosoever." "Whosoever shall call on the name of the Lord shall be saved." I hope I have not diminished the range of the text ; certainly I have not intended to do so. Mind that none of you shut the door in your own faces. I want each one to come in, and find salvation at once. For the time being you may forget the Negro, the Red Indian, and the "heathen Chinee"; but I beseech you do not forget to come to Jesus yourself. Come, for you may come, you should come, you must come.

> "None are excluded hence but those
>   Who do themselves exclude ;
> Welcome the learned and polite,
>   The ignorant and rude.
> While grace most freely saves the prince,
>   The poor may take their share ;
> No mortal has a just pretence
>   To perish in despair."

There is the text "Whosoever shall call on the name of the Lord shall be delivered," or "saved." Believe it, and obey it. It is a gracious gift; take it, and be rich for ever.

Furthermore, *the requirement is very plain.* "Whosoever shall call on the name of the Lord." You do not need a library to explain to you how you can be saved. Here it is—"Call on the name of the Lord." This is "The Plain Man's Pathway to heaven." You will not need to go to the Sorbonne at Paris, nor to the University of Oxford, to be tutored in the art of finding salvation. Believe and live. Is not that plain enough? "Whosoever shall call on the name of the Lord shall be saved." What does calling upon the name of the Lord mean ? To call on the name of the Lord means, first, to *believe in God as he reveals himself in Scripture.* His revelation of himself is his "name." If you make a god of your own, you have no promise that he will save you: on the contrary, if you make him, he will be good for nothing, for he will be less than yourself. If you are now willing to come to the light, and see the Lord as he displays himself in his own Word, then you shall know a great God and a Saviour. You are not merely to believe in *a* god, but in the living and true God : in Jehovah, the God of Abraham, of Isaac, and of Jacob, the God and Father of our Lord and Saviour Jesus Christ. If you accept him as being what he states himself to be, in him you shall find salvation. The pity of it is that the most of people in these days worship a god of their own invention. They do not make an image of clay, or of gold, but they construct a deity in their minds according to their own thoughts. They proudly judge as to what God ought to be, and they will not receive God as he really is. What is this but a god-making as gross as that which is performed by the heathen? What can be more wicked than to attempt to imagine a better god than the one true and living God? As the deity of your fancy has no existence, I would not recommend you to trust in him. There is one living and true God, and that living God has revealed himself in the two Books of the Old and New Testament. In these he is more clearly seen than in his works of creation or of providence. *In this God you must trust;* and if you trust him, he will not deceive you. "Blessed are all they that put their trust in him." If you trust in "thought," or "progress," or any other deity of your own making, you will perish; but if you rely upon the living God, he will not, cannot, forsake you. Trust in Father, Son, and Holy Ghost, and you shall be delivered. "He that believeth on him shall not be confounded." A simple, child-like trust in God as he reveals himself in his Word, and especially as he unveils himself in the blessed person of the Lord Jesus Christ, will save you. In the Lord Jesus dwelleth all the fulness of the Godhead bodily; trust in him, and you are saved.

To call on the name of the Lord also means to pray. That is the idea which naturally arises to the mind at the first sound of the word. You are lost in a wood. What are you to do? You are to *call* for help. "O God, hear my cry! Deliver me, for my trust is in thee!" If I compare you to a wandering sheep, what can you do? You cannot find your way back to the fold; the brambles hold you fast, and tear your flesh. Well, you can *bleat*, and thus call for the Shepherd. Prayer,—real, sincere, believing prayer will never fail. The Lord has said, "Call upon me in the day of trouble, and I will deliver thee."

I recollect, in the time of my soul-trouble, how I lived on this text for months. It only looks like a lozenge, but it is made of the essence of meat, and it will sustain life for many a day. Try the power of it. "Whosoever shall call on the name of the Lord shall be saved." I said to myself,—"I do call on his name; and I will continue to call on his name: yea, if I perish, I will pray, and perish only there!" Nor did I call upon the Lord in supplication in vain. He heard me, and saved me. Blessed be his holy name! Praying, believing, trusting, none can fail of salvation. The requirement is very plain,—"Trust and pray."

And when you have done this, then remember that *to call upon the name of the Lord means also to confess that name.* We read in the Old Testament, "Then began men to call upon the name of the Lord." Not that they then first prayed, but they then began to meet together avowedly to worship Jehovah. They came out from among men, and named the sacred name as that of their God and Lord; declaring that, whatever others did, they would serve him. The Lord requires all saved ones to do this. You must confess that the Lord is your God, and Jesus is your Saviour. You must say, "This God is our God for ever and ever." Our Lord put it, "He that believeth and is baptized shall be saved." Paul saith, "With the heart man believeth unto righteousness, and with the mouth confession is made unto salvation." You must, in some way or other, confess your faith; and the best way is that which the Lord has himself ordained, saying, "Thus it becometh us to fulfil all righteousness." No longer wishing to live without God, no longer trusting to what you can see, and hear, and do, you must henceforth place your whole reliance upon God alone, and own the Lord as your God and Father. No man doing this shall be left to perish. Out of temporal and eternal troubles you shall be delivered. God will help you all your life long if you trust him. "He shall cover thee with his feathers, and under his wings shalt thou trust, his truth shall be thy shield and buckler." Whosoever trusts, prays, and avows himself to be on the Lord's side, shall be saved.

This requirement is simple enough, and I do not see what less could be asked of any man. Would you have a man saved who will not trust his God? Would you have a man forgiven who will not obey his Lord? Has Christ come into the world to pander to our sin, and save us while we continue in rebellion? God forbid! His grace is manifested to make us own God in everything, and walk before the Lord in the land of the living. This also the Holy Ghost works in us to will and to do.

I will spend a minute or two in reminding you that, as the requirement is plain, so *the assurance of blessing is positive.* "Whosoever shall call on the name of the Lord *shall* be delivered," or "saved." In this there are no provisos and peradventures. The text is not a bare hope, but a solemn assertion. If thou believest, poor soul, though thou art altogether a mass of sin, thou shalt be saved! Do you not see how sure it is? God, who cannot lie, pledges his word to you: risk your soul on it. Indeed, there is no risk. The only hope I have this day is in the promise of my faithful God which he makes to those who call upon his name. I dare not rest anywhere else, but on his bare word I gladly venture my eternal all. How can it be that a sincere trust in God's own promise can ever be rejected of the Lord? Sitting by the bedside of a dying man, who was resting in Christ even as I am, I said to myself—Suppose we, who trust alone in Jesus, should perish, what then? Why, it would be to the everlasting dishonour of the Lord in whom we trusted. We should lose our souls certainly, but he would lose his honour. Think of one of us being able to say in hell, "I trusted in the boasted Saviour's aid, and rested myself on God, and yet I am lost." Sirs, heaven itself would be darkened, and the crown jewels of God would lose their lustre, if that could once be the case! But it cannot be. If you trust in the Lord God Almighty, he will save you as surely as he is God. No one shall ever think better of God than he is. Open your mouth as wide as you will, and he will fill it.

And now, to wind up as to the proclamation: remember that, although it is so far-reaching as to embrace a wide world of believers, yet *it is a personal message to you* at this hour. "Whosoever" includes *yourself;* and if you see it from the right angle, it peculiarly looks at *you. You,* calling upon God, shall be saved ; *you,* even YOU! Friend, I do not know your name, nor do I need to know it ; but I mean this word for *you. You* shall be saved if *you* call upon the name of the Lord. "Ah!" you say, "I wish my name was written down in the Bible." Would it comfort you at all? If it were written in the Scripture, "Charles Haddon Spurgeon shall be saved," I am afraid I should not get much comfort out of the promise, for I should go home, and fetch out the London Directory, and see if there was not another person of that name, or very like it. How much worse would it be for the Smiths and the

Browns! No, my brethren, do not ask to see your name in the inspired volume; but be content with what you do see, namely, your character! When the Scripture says, "Whosoever," you cannot shut yourself out of that. Since it is written, "Whosoever shall call on the name of the Lord shall be saved," call on that name, and grasp the blessing. Despair itself can scarcely evade the comfort of this blessed text. O Holy Spirit, the Comforter, seal it upon each heart!

But perhaps you have not called upon the name of the Lord. Then begin at once. Cry, "Lord, have mercy upon me!" and cry after that sort immediately. If you have never prayed, pray now. May God the Holy Spirit lead you to call upon the name of the Lord at this exact moment, without waiting to go home, or to get into another room! Though you have never believed in the Lord Jesus before, believe in him now. If this be the first breath of faith that you have ever breathed, the promise is as sure to you as it is to those of us who have known the Lord these forty years. "Whosoever shall call on the name of the Lord shall be saved," is a word to a careless fellow who has never prayed in his life.

O my hearer, the text speaks to you. How I wish I could get at you, and take you by the hand, and hold you till I had made you think! I remember when Mr. Richard Weaver preached at Park Street Chapel, in his younger days, he came down from the pulpit, and ran over the pews to get at the people, that he might speak to them individually, and say, "you," and "you," and "you." I am not nimble enough on my legs to do *that*, and I do not think I should try it if I were younger; but I wish I could, somehow or other, come to each one of you, and press home these glad tidings of great joy. *You*, my dear old friend, it means *you! You*, young woman, over there to the right, it means *you! You*, dear child, sitting with your grandmother, it means *you!* "Whosoever shall call on the name of the Lord shall be saved." O Lord, bless this word to every unconverted person to whom it comes!

II. I could almost wish to close with this soft music, but I dare not maim a text. I will deal with the second part of it with exceeding brevity, but I dare not silence it altogether. The second portion of the text contains AN INSTRUCTIVE DECLARATION. "It shall come to pass that whosoever shall call on the name of the Lord shall be delivered." That was abundantly fulfilled at Pentecost, for on that day a great multitude believed, and were baptized, and were saved: thus those who called on the name of the Lord were delivered. But listen, "In mount Zion and in Jerusalem shall be deliverance." This also was literally true: the first preaching of the gospel was to the Jews at Jerusalem itself. Salvation came to mount Zion, and to the city of the great King. The fountain for sin and for uncleanness was opened at Jerusalem.

There is something about that fact which strikes me very solemnly this morning; for though this deliverance came to some, yet the city was totally destroyed. The kingdom of heaven came near them, but they put it away, and they were overthrown with a fearful destruction. The Jews had long been outwardly the Lord's chosen people, but in a measure he had cast them off, for the Romans ruled the land, and they in their wilful blindness crucified their King. The favoured nation nailed the Messiah to the tree; and yet to Jerusalem sinners, salvation was first preached. Salvation was of the Jews, and by Jews it was brought to us Gentiles. Sad calamity that they should bring us life, and yet as a nation sink down to spiritual death!

Notice that the prophet says, "In mount Zion and in Jerusalem shall be deliverance, as the Lord hath said." He promised deliverance, and he sent it according to his word: if *they* would not have it, he sent it as he said, and their blood was on their own heads when they refused it. The Lord went to the full length of his mercy in sending salvation to those leaders of iniquity, who with wicked hands had crucified their own Messiah.

As a result of the Lord's goodness, a remnant was saved. Notice it, "and in the remnant whom the Lord shall call." A remnant did call upon the Lord and live. Those eleven that stood up at Pentecost, and bore witness to the resurrection, were all Jews; and those who met in the upper room, when the Holy Ghost came down, were Jews: this was the remnant. But the solemn thought is that it was only a remnant of God's favoured people. Centuries of visitations, prophets, miracles; yet only a remnant saved! God's Shekinah shining out among them; and yet only a remnant obedient! The very Christ of God born of their nation; and yet only a remnant saved! To this day we utter the truth when we sing—

> "Ye chosen seed of Israel's race,
> A remnant weak and small."

The Jewish church is a very insignificant portion of the Jewish people. The apostle tells us that "at this present time there is a remnant according to the election of grace"; and Isaiah says, "Except the Lord of hosts had left unto us a very small remnant, we should have been as Sodom, and we should have been like unto Gomorrah." Poor Israel, poor Israel! Most favoured for many an age, and yet only a remnant brought to call upon the saving Lord! Many come from distant lands, and sit down with Abraham, and Isaac, and Jacob in the kingdom of God; but the children of the kingdom are cast out into outer darkness,—all but a mere remnant.

To my mind it is most instructive to notice that even that remnant never called upon the name of the Lord until the Lord called upon them,—"The remnant whom the Lord shall call." We all of us need a miracle of grace to make us perform the simple act of calling upon God. This was manifestly true in the case of Israel, for as a nation it rejected Jesus of Nazareth, and only a few were converted by the power of the Holy Ghost. But whether Jews or Greeks, we are similarly depraved; and unless effectual calling shall call us out of our natural state, the very last thing that we shall ever do will be to come to Jesus, and to rest in him. Unhappy condition, to refuse the highest good!

Believing Jews are a remnant to this day, and only here and there is one called by grace. You say, "What have we to do with that?" We have much to do with it. Let us pray for our Lord's own countrymen. Let us labour for them. This also let us do: let us learn from their fall. O you that are children of godly parents, you that habitually attend places of worship, you who sit in this house of prayer year after year—you are much in the same position as Israel of old!

Yours are the outward privileges, will you reject the hopes which they set before you? My fear is lest you should get so accustomed to hearing the gospel that you should think that mere hearing is enough. I tremble lest you should grow so habituated to the externals of religion that you should be dead to all the internal parts of it, and only a remnant of you should be saved. Think of the multitudes in England who hear the gospel, and of the comparatively few who are called by grace to come and believe in Jesus Christ. It is sorrowful to think of the breadth of gospel grace and the narrowness of man's acceptance of it. The feast is great; the guests are few. I see an ocean of mercy without a shore; and on it there floats an ark wherein but few are saved. Shall it be always so? Oh, come, and receive the gift of free grace! Alas! I see men sunk in the darkness of unbelief, and only a remnant rising to the light of faith! Altogether, in this London, out of four or five millions, we have not half a million at worship at any one time! Out of that half million, how many do you think are real Christians? Truly, it is a remnant still. Oh, that you and I may be of that remnant!

Let us further pray the Lord to gather in the multitude, and so to accomplish speedily the number of his elect. Oh, that he would not only magnify the sovereignty of his grace, but reveal the largeness of it! Oh, that he would give the well-beloved Jesus to see of the travail of his soul till he is satisfied! O Lord, the oxen and the fatlings are killed, and all things are ready; let it not be again reported that those who are bidden are not worthy! Or, if it be so, enable us to go out into the highways and hedges and compel the outcasts to come in, that the wedding may be furnished with guests! Go forth, ye messengers of Christ, into all the world! Rise up, my brothers and sisters, from this service, and go forth, every one of you, to call in as many as you find; yea, to compel them to come in! May the Lord cause that in London, and in Britain, there may be deliverance; yea, may his salvation be made known unto the ends of the earth! Amen.

The Lord's Own Salvation

"But I will have mercy upon the house of Judah, and will save them by the Lord their God, and will not save them by bow, nor by sword, nor by battle, by horses, nor by horsemen."—Hosea i. 7.

GOD *is very considerate towards the messengers by whom he delivers his word to men.* They are bound to deliver his word faithfully, whatever the tidings may be. Sometimes the burden of the Lord is very heavy. The prophets have to denounce woe upon woe, with terrible monotony of threatening; and then it is that God hastens to relieve them by giving them a gracious word, so that they may refresh their hearts, and not be altogether crushed beneath their load. We have an instance here of the Lord's care for his heralds. Hosea was bound to say, in the name of the Lord, "I will no more have mercy upon the house of Israel; but I will utterly take them away"; but when he had said *that,* with heavy heart and tearful eye, he was allowed to add, "But I will have mercy upon the house of Judah." The Lord will not let our spirit fail beneath a burden which is all of grief; but he will grant us the high privilege of proclaiming grace, as well as publishing judgment. Dear brethren in Christ, if you have to preach God's word, preach it faithfully, and abate no syllable of its stern threatenings. Woe unto him who is afraid to preach the terrors of the Lord! Woe unto the man who refuses to put his hand into the bitter box, and take out the wormwood and gall which make such salutary medicine for the souls of men! We must at times speak lightning, and prove ourselves sons of thunder. We must bring on the storm and tempest in the heart of man, if fair summertide discoursing will not touch them. For the most of men there is no going to heaven except by Weeping Cross; and we must drive them that way with God's thundering sentences of judgment. Let us lead them by the path of sorrow to the Man of sorrows, sorrowing ourselves because it is so hard to bring them to a godly sorrow. It is at our soul's peril that we allow a warning to lie silent. "If the watchman warn them not, they shall perish ; but their blood will I require at the watchman's hands." Let us think of that, and give ourselves up to our Master's work, even when it is heaviest, cheered by the fact that we have to speak of such glorious truths, such precious promises, such a gracious Christ, such a free salvation, such full pardon for the very chief of sinners, such abundant help for those that have no strength, such fatherly compassion to those that are out of the way. Our themes of joy by far outweigh our topics of grief, and we find the Lord's service a happy one.

The connection of our text suggests the thought that *there is a limit to the long-suffering of God.* He bade Hosea say, " I will no more have mercy upon Israel." He had borne with that guilty people very long, and overlooked their daring crimes ; but he would do so no longer : he would give them over to the enemy, who would carry them quite away, so that Israel as a distinct monarchy should cease to be. O my hearers, God is very gracious, but his Spirit shall not always strive with you. A little more sin, and you may be over the boundary, and God may give you up. Stay, I pray you ! Do not further provoke. Repent, and turn unto the Lord with full purpose of heart.

Having made that observation, I would make another, namely, that *the Lord makes distinctions among guilty men according to the sovereignty of his grace.* " I will no more have mercy upon the house of Israel ; but I will have mercy upon the house of Judah." Had not Judah sinned too ? Might not the Lord have given up Judah also ! Indeed he might justly have done so, but he delighteth in mercy. Many sin, and righteously bring upon themselves the punishment due to sin : they believe not in Christ, and die in their sins. But God has mercy, according to the greatness of his heart, upon multitudes who could not be saved on any other footing but that of undeserved mercy. Claiming his royal right he says, " I will have mercy on whom I will have mercy." The prerogative of mercy is vested in the sovereignty of God : that prerogative he exercises. He gives where he pleases, and he has a right to do so, since none have any claim upon him. We are all under his rule, and by that rule we are under condemnation ; and if he should leave us there, it would be strictly just ; but if any be saved it is an act of pure, undeserved grace, for which he is to have all the praise.

Note, too, that even in the darkest times, when whole nations go astray from him, *he still reserves unto himself a people.* " I will no more have mercy upon the house of Israel ; but I will have mercy upon the house of Judah, and will save them." God will have a people even when those who are called his people prove unworthy of the name. There never was a night so dark but that God had a star shining through its blackness. There never was a desert so drear but God could lead a people through it, and make the wilderness rejoice. There never shall be a time in which Christ will not have a remnant according to the election of grace, who will maintain his truth and the honour of his name. Let us be comforted by this, and look for brighter and better times, however dark the days may seem to be just now. God will save his own, and by his own will keep his glory bright among men.

But now the text brings us to consider this fact, that *God will save his own people in his own way.* He tells us positively how he will save the house of Judah, and negatively how he will not save them. "I will have mercy upon the house of Judah, and will save them by the Lord their God, and will not save them by bow, nor by sword, nor by battle, by horses, nor by horsemen." God displays his sovereignty not only in the persons saved, but in the ways whereby that salvation is wrought out.

The point which we shall consider is God's way of saving his people, as instanced in the text; and we remark, first, *that oftentimes God puts visible means aside in dealing with his people:* "Not by bow, nor by sword, nor by battle, by horses, nor by horsemen." Secondly, he has *good reasons for doing this:* he acts with infinite wisdom. Thirdly, *there is a gospel in this,* a gospel which has special relation to us. Oh, for a blessing from the Spirit of the Lord!

I. First, then, GOD IS PLEASED VERY OFTEN, IN WORKING SALVATION, TO PUT MEANS ASIDE. He said of Israel, "I will break the bow of Israel in the valley of Jezreel." He thus struck out of the hands of his people their only defence; they had trusted in their bow, and the Lord destroyed it.

First, *the Lord does this in the work of salvation by grace.* Salvation is of the Lord alone. Salvation is not of human merit, for there is no such thing. Plenty of demerit you can find anywhere and everywhere, but of merit there is none. "When we have done all, we are unprofitable servants: we have done no more than it was our duty to have done." But we have not done all. Alas! on the contrary, we have done those things which we ought not to have done; and we have left undone the things which we ought to have done, and there is no health in us. In ourselves we have neither health, help, nor hope. We are not, we cannot be, saved by our works. We dismiss the idea with an honest indignation, each one of us for himself. Neither are we saved by any good dispositions which lie dormant and latent within us, for there are no such things. There is none good, no not one. The heart is, in every case, deceitful, and desperately wicked. Who can bring a clean thing out of an unclean? Not one. If our salvation depended upon our hearts going after God of themselves, and the motions of our nature ascending towards the Most High of themselves, it would be a hopeless case. But divine grace waiteth not for man, neither tarrieth for the sons of men. When we were yet without strength, in due time Christ died for the ungodly. "You hath he quickened, who were dead in trespasses and in sins." The first movement is from God to us, not from us to God. As soon expect the darkness to create the day as expect the sinner to turn his own heart to the Lord. We are saved by the Lord's grace, not by our works, nor by our feelings, nor by our desires, nor even by our sense of need. I believe it is one object of God's infinite wisdom in each individual case to make this doctrine clear to the understanding and the heart. Certainly it is one object of every faithful ministry. We preach down the creature, and preach up the Saviour. Yet, preach as we may, self-righteousness is so natural to man, self-trust is so congenial to our proud imbecility, that we cannot get it out of men till the Holy Spirit comes. Every man his own Saviour is the kind of doctrine which is popular; but to set aside our own doings is to offend many. I see before me a picture which was once before the mind of Isaiah. Our nature seems like a rainbow-coloured field of grass in the early days of summer. The golden kingcups are inter- mingled with flowers of every hue. What a luxuriant garden! Wait a moment! A wind comes—a hot sirocco burns its deadly way. "The grass withereth, the flower fadeth: because the spirit of the Lord bloweth upon it: surely the people is grass." So have we seen men glorious in their own self-righteousness, boastful of their moral purity and we have half thought, surely there is something in all this! We walk over the same field after the withering work of the Holy Ghost has been there, and men have been convinced of sin, and we see nothing but disappointment, and hear nothing but confession of failure. We see no flowers, but dead, withered grass. How soon has the glory departed! The comeliness of the field is passed away as in the twinkling of an eye!

You cannot have forgotten, some of you, when this terrible self- withering happened to you. When God's rebukes corrected you, your beauty passed away as the moth. Before I was instructed as to myself I thought myself as good a fellow as could be found within fifty miles; but when the Spirit of God had revealed me to myself, I thought myself the basest creature within five hundred miles; or, for the matter of that, even outside or inside of hell itself. You may, perhaps, have seen a picture drawn by a cunning artist. It represents a lady, very fair and beautiful to look upon; but the picture is so contrived that you discover underneath it the form of death. That which appeared outwardly so lovely is only a veiled skeleton. Just that kind of change the Spirit of God makes upon our moral beauty: he turns it into cor- ruption by making us see what we really are. The bones of the skeleton of depraved nature stand out through the proud flesh of our self-righteous pride. Then we cry to God for mercy. Then we give up all idea of saving ourselves. Neither bow, nor sword, nor horse, nor horsemen, are any longer our confidence. The weapons of our self-help are looked upon by us as weapons of rebellion—and they really are so; and we throw them away, and will have nothing further to do with them. The man upon whom there is found a bad coin is very earnest in declaring that it is none of his, somebody must have slipped it into his pocket. He will not own it. A little while ago he thought to himself, "What a splendid imitation it is! How well I have cheated the Queen!" Self-righteousness is nothing but a piece of counterfeit coin; and when all goes well with us, we say, "How well I have done it! How splendid is my righteousness!" But when the Spirit of God arrests us, then we are anxious to get rid of the very thing wherein we gloried. What was our righteousness we reckon to be as filthy rags—and we reckon according to truth. Thus God saves us, not by bow, nor by sword, nor by battle, nor by horses, nor by horsemen, but by his grace, which comes to us freely when Jesus is made of God unto us wisdom, righteousness, sanctification, and redemption.

It is so in the actual salvation of men, and *it is often so in their calling to this salvation.* Was any man ever converted in the way in which he expected to be? I hardly think so. I know what you thought would happen; at least I know what many expect. They look for an interesting incident. They suppose, perhaps, that they will have a very wonderful dream; or that, going to hear a minister, there will be something very striking in the sermon which will alarm or depress them, so that they will be tempted to commit suicide, or do some other outrageous thing. Possibly, on the other hand, they half expect that there will happen a sudden death in the family, or sickness upon many, and that so they will be impressed; or, possibly, like Martin Luther with his friend Alexis, they may be walking out in a thunder-storm, and Alexis will be killed, and they will be aroused in that way. I, myself, always looked for something very remarkable, but it did not come to me. And yet something happened which was more remarkable than the most remarkable thing would have been: I simply heard the gospel command, "Look unto me, and be ye saved." I looked and I lived; and that is all the story I have to tell you. Dear hearer, that is all the story, very likely, you will ever have to tell. You have come in here to-night, and perhaps you have even desired that something very wonderful may take place. Nothing of the sort may happen, and yet the infinite mercy of God may visit your heart and sweetly melt it. Or ever you are aware, you may say to yourself—

> "I do believe, I will believe,
> That Jesus died for me";

and, on a sudden, that change will come over you of which you have so often heard—by no means the physical change which you have looked for, the extravagant delirium of sorrow struggling with delight. You will simply drop into the arms of Christ, and rest in his great sacrifice, and find peace. That will be all. You will not be saved by bow, nor by sword, nor by battle, nor by horses, nor by horsemen, but by a simple trust in the Lord alone. What more do you want? What more can you hope to receive?

I feel very grateful to God whenever a person attributes his conversion to me. I feel both honoured and humbled. But if you are brought to the Lord Jesus, and no word of mine shall be used, but only that still small voice which speaks in solemn silence to the heart, I shall be equally pleased, so long as you are saved. If hungry souls receive the bread of heaven, I will not fret because they took it from some other hand than mine. Oh, that even now the Lord himself might come like the dew which falls in its own special way, and may he refresh your hearts unto eternal life, and fulfil this word: "I will save them by the Lord their God, and will not save them by bow, nor by sword, nor by battle, by horses, nor by horsemen."

In the next place, the same thing is true with regard to *the progress of religion, and the work of revivals.* Let every man work as he feels called to do, provided he follows the rules of his Lord; but we have seen revivals of which it was said at the first, "We will get up a revival." Revivals can be got up, but are they worth the trouble? What has been the end of them all? A few years after, the result, where is it? I hear an echo say, "Where is it?" I cannot tell you what has become of it; in many cases I fear that the disappointed church has become more hard to stir than it was before. Brethren, I hopefully believe that there will soon come a deep, widespread, lasting revival of religion, and it may be it will come just as it used to in apostolic times. How did they act in Jerusalem? What did they do throughout Asia Minor? What was the apostles' plan? I cannot find, for the life of me, that they did anything else but preach the gospel, while at the same time they went from house to house, and held meetings for prayer; and thus the kingdom of Christ came. They did not work up a revival, but they prayed it down. They simply waited upon the Lord in supplication and service. They might have tried other plans had they been so unwise as to think of them. They would never have tolerated the dodges of the present period, the adaptations of the gospel, and the degrading of it, by secular lectures, entertainments, and so forth. They never dreamed of keeping abreast of the times with liberal philosophical teaching; but I recollect that Paul was so resolutely ignorant as to say, "I determined not to know anything among you, save Jesus Christ, and him crucified." Standing all together the chosen preachers of the first days could aver—"We preach Christ crucified." They could all say *that*, and say it emphatically. All the men of the college of the apostles stuck to that theme; and see the effect!

> "Nations, the learned and the rude,
> Were by these heavenly arms subdued,
> While Satan raging at his loss,
> Abhorred the doctrine of the cross."

I wish all the churches would try this old way again, for it seems to me that the world will never be subdued to Christ by the wooden sword of reason, but only by the true Jerusalem blade of a gospel revealed from heaven. Until we take up such methods as our Lord has ordained, and make our sole confidence to be in the Lord our God, who "will not save by bow, nor by sword, nor by battle, by horses, nor by horsemen," we shall never see great results. Grand preaching, fine preaching, eloquent preaching! Yes; but the apostle was afraid of it, lest the faith of his converts should stand in the wisdom of men. Though he could have spoken with the tongue of an orator, he did not use the wisdom of words, lest the cross of Christ should be of none effect.

"But, surely," cries one, "we must have some advancement in theology. We ought to know more than our old fathers did." This is the pride of our hearts. Would you advance beyond the apostles? Into what can you advance but into the ditch of error? They did not crave for an advance in the apostolic times; but they were satisfied to speak over again "all the words of this life." They remained true to the "faith once for all delivered to the saints," and they found salvation in this primitive revelation. Why should we go gadding elsewhere? Depend upon it God will not save men by advanced thought, nor by eloquent discoursings, nor by literary beauties: he "will save them by the Lord their God, and will not save them by bow, nor by sword, nor by battle, by horses, nor by horsemen."

I believe that the same great truth will be made apparent *as to the establishment of the truth of God in this land.* How my soul has been burdened with the many that have turned aside, and the few that remain faithful to the covenant God of Israel! These last are not so very few as some would make them out to be, but yet they are sadly scant in number. God has reserved unto himself seven thousand that have not bowed their knee to Baal. Oh, that there were a thousand times as many! But we have striven with all our might to bear our outspoken testimony for the old faith, and we have hopefully thought, that many would rally to the cry; but it is not so, nor, perhaps, is it God's mind that it should be. Men of eminence have held their tongues, and brethren once ardent for the gospel have practically gone over to the enemy. I am sure that the Lord will confound the adversary, and bring forth his truth as the noonday; but it may not be as we would suggest. He has his own way; let us watch for him to make bare his arm. Perhaps those who are faithful must stand alone, must bear their witness in solitary places, and be the objects of general derision. Perhaps for many a year the heavenly fire will only smoulder amidst the ashes. But it is all right; truth shall hold the crown of the causeway yet, and Christ's own word shall lift its head from the waves that have washed over it, and be the fairer for the washing; for the truth hath God's might with it, and it must prevail. He "will save them by the Lord their God, and will not save them by bow, nor by sword, nor by battle, by horses, nor by horsemen." We must be content to subside; to be nothing; to be never heard of; to die. So be it if the truth shall live. This will be better than if we formed a numerous band, and carried everything by majorities, and set up a strong party, and won the day: for then man might be great, and God be forgotten, but now he shall be all in all. When you have seen how I fail, and those that are with me, and how plans and efforts are futile, you will all the more clearly see what the Lord can do.

Dear friends, I would make one other application of these words, and I trust it may be profitable to you. *The text has a voice to God's people in the day of trouble.* I may be addressing godly people who are in most terrible distress. You have faith in God that he will bring you out of your affliction. Maintain that faith; and if for a long time no deliverance should come, still maintain it. Perhaps you have hopes from a certain quarter. Those hopes may come to nothing: that cistern will leak. You have another friend to whom you can apply. Yes, you can apply; that is all that will happen, for that tank also holds no water. When you have tried all the cisterns, be wise enough to recollect the fountain. It may be that there will come a day when every door will be fast closed, and you will see no way of relief whatever; but bethink you that then there will remain the one way, which you should have followed at the first. In such an hour let my text speak with you: "He will save them by the Lord their God, and he will not save them by bow, nor by sword, nor by battle, by horses, nor by horsemen." What a glorious vision is that of Jehovah alone with his own right hand getting to himself the victory! When Israel came out of Egypt, what armies vanquished

Pharaoh? Who fought on Israel's side to bring them out of Egypt? Nobody. Then there was no human victor to extol, no human warrior to praise; but clear and plain the hymn rang out—"Sing unto the Lord, for he hath triumphed gloriously." If there had been an ally with God the glory might have been divided; but as it was, the Lord alone was exalted in that day. When Israel fought with Amalek it is evident that the battle never depended upon their fighting, for—

> "While Moses stood with arms spread wide,
> Success was found on Israel's side;
> But when through weariness they failed,
> That moment Amalek prevailed!"

so that the real fighting was done by those uplifted hands that brought down the divine success, and made Joshua mighty in the battle. When Israel crossed the Jordan, and came into the promised land to fight the Canaanites, the very first conquest was that of Jericho. Did they bring battering-rams to the walls? Did they gradually throw down the structure with their axes and picks? Oh, no! they compassed the city seven days, and God made the walls to fall when the people gave a shout. In the memorable deliverances of God's people, God has said to the second cause, "Stand back; let my glory come to the front." The bow, the sword, the battle, the horses, and the horsemen, he has sent them all about their business; and then the Lord their God has led the van, and his enemies have been scattered like the dust of the threshing-floor. When he takes up the quarrel of his covenant he makes short work of it, for "the Lord is a man of war; Jehovah is his name;" and when he lays bare his arm to defend the cause of his people, he wants no helpers. Now can you lean on the Lord? Can you grasp the Invisible? Can you lean *alone* on God, and forego all helpers? Can you grasp his bared arm, and let all things else go? O man of God, if thou canst, thou shalt glorify God, and thou shalt surely be delivered! If thou must have thy bow and thy sword, or else give up hope, then the battle rests with thyself. How canst thou plead the promise of God? But when thou puttest the bow aside, and the sword is hung on the wall, then canst thou go to him who is better to thee than bow and sword, and rest in him, and he will work gloriously, so that his own name shall be magnified, and thou shalt be blessed. I pray the Holy Spirit to apply that truth to any heart here that is heavy by reason of sore conflict at this time. Oh, for grace to rest in the Lord and wait patiently for him, for in his own time and way he will work, and none shall hinder him.

So much upon our first point, that oftentimes God puts the means aside in dealing with his people.

II. But now, secondly, God has GOOD REASONS FOR THIS. I shall very briefly touch upon this theme. The Lord is full of wisdom, and his doings are ever prudent. He always has good reasons for everything, but one of the things we should never do is, to ask his reasons. It is an unreasonable thing to ask God to give reasons for what he does. His answer to arrogant questioners is—"May I not do as I will with my own?" Oh for grace to be silent where God is silent! Is he not God, and we worms of the dust? Who shall presume to ask him why or what he does? Better far to say, "It is the Lord, let him do what seemeth him good." If he never gave us a reason for what he did, we ought to be well content to leave all with him, knowing that he must do that which is best and wisest.

But, so far as in humility we may dare to look, we have looked, and we believe that the Lord's ways are intended, first, *to prevent all boasting*. How prone we are to self-esteem! How wickedly we rob God to honour ourselves! If God uses *us*—if God uses any sort of means—yet there is no credit to the means which he uses, but to himself only. I read the other day of a certain writer who says, "I wrote the four hundred pages of this book with one pen." Where is that pen? Does anybody want it? If it were advertised as an exhibition, I should not go to see it. I care a deal more for the hand that wrote, and for what was written, than for the pen with which it was written. A common goose-quill it was in the case referred to, and no more. Ah, how plainly can we see where the quill came from! God uses men for a certain purpose, as we use a hammer, or a saw, or a gimlet. Suppose that when we had done with such tools, and put them back into the box, they all began to cry, "See what we have done! What a sharp saw I was! What a heavy hammer I was! Did I not hit the nail on the head?" Such boastings would be foolishness. Shall the axe boast itself against him that heweth therewith? We do not judge that the instrument ought to take credit to itself; but it does so in our case whenever it can, and this is a great injury to us. Some of us might have enjoyed a much larger blessing, if we had not grown top-heavy with the blessing we already enjoyed. God saved a soul or two by you, my dear friend, and you began to rub your hands, and think that you were something better than an angel. You were running away with God's glory, and thus ending your own influence. Often this is the cause of the drying up of hopeful usefulness. The instrument began to exalt itself, and so the Lord put up the bow, the sword, the horses, and the horsemen, and then all men saw what powerless things these were. Oh, that the Lord may never feel compelled to leave you and me to ourselves! Oh, that he may deign to honour us by using us to his glory. I had far rather die than stand a withered tree in the vineyard of the Lord, and yet, what better should I be if he withdrew the dew of his grace from me?

Next, he does this *to take us off from all reliance upon second causes and outward means*. You people of God, the process of weaning is, with you, full often a long and tedious one; but if ever it is accomplished, your faith will rejoice, even as Abraham made a great feast at Isaac's weaning.

My dear hearers, some of you are not saved yet, and I will tell you what happens with many of you. You come here on Sabbath days, and to Monday prayer-meetings, and Thursday services, and I am glad to see you. You also read your Bibles; I am glad of that. You say a thing you call a prayer: I do not know whether I am glad about *that*. But I will tell you what you are doing. You are making yourselves quite comfortable, as if, by some singular process, salvation would insensibly penetrate you by your being found in good company, hearing the Word, and so on. Let me remind you that these things were never prescribed as the way of salvation. I do not want you to run away from hearing the Word, or from the use of the means; but I do want to assure you that, if you trust in these means, you will be disappointed in the result. These are mere pitchers, but they will not quench your thirst if there is no water in them. Look to God, not to your minister. Get to Jesus himself rather than to the sacred Book. Remember how the Saviour puts it—for this is not a wrested reading—"Ye search the Scriptures; for in them ye think ye have eternal life: but ye will not come to me that ye might have life." Pass beyond the Scriptures to the Christ whom the Scriptures reveal. Do not stay in the porch of the Word, but enter the house of the truth itself, which is Christ Jesus. It is not singing hymns and saying prayers; it is getting to the Lord in praise and really coming to Christ in prayer. I wish you not to stay away from any of the services; I wish you to be where the means may be blessed to you; but the means of themselves cannot save you. There is nothing in preaching—there is nothing in public service that can mechanically bring salvation to you; and do not expect it. "Ye must be born again!" You must distinctly go to Christ for yourselves, for the Lord saves men by the Lord Jesus Christ, and he will not save them by books, and prayer-meetings, and sermons any more than he would save Judah by the bow, the sword, the battle, the horses, and the horsemen. The Lord set aside horse and horsemen to bring the people to himself; and often he lays people up so that they cannot get out to hear the minister, or he drafts them away to some portion of the country where they get no sermon, that then they may go to the God of all true sermons, and may find salvation in Jesus Christ himself.

Again, beloved, the Lord blesses his people himself *that he may endear himself to them.* He reveals himself to them apart from other things, that they may see *him* and know what *he* can do. You do not know to the full what God can do so long as he keeps within the bounds of the ordinary means, or you feel that you are well provided for by ordinary methods. You are apt to forget that *God* provides for you, because your quarterly allowance is received so regularly. Now, suppose that your business fails. Ah! then God must provide for you: then you will see what God is doing. Suppose that, instead of being in one place, you should be kicked about like a football, and still the Lord should give you rest in himself: then you will see what he can do. When we are in fine feather, and everybody is kind to us, we hardly know the lovingkindness of the Lord, it is so smothered up by secondary agencies. When we get quite alone, and nobody is kind to us, and we approach to the Lord in solitary trust, and prove his power to comfort us, then we know more of what he is in himself to his people. The night reveals the stars, and sorrow and loneliness manifest the Lord's presence. But, beloved, God does this to endear himself to us, that seeing more of him we may love him more, and may say to ourselves, "What a gracious God he is to take notice of me, to interpose for me, to come and, by his own mighty power, do for me what the ordinary ways and means fail to do!" In this way also the Lord often gives a double blessing—a blessing in the gift, and a blessing in the way of giving.

Now look at Hezekiah's case. Supposing Hezekiah had gone out to fight Sennacherib, and had defeated him, a certain number of the inhabitants of Jerusalem would have been killed in the battle; but when the Lord delivered Hezekiah without a battle, then there were no funerals in Jerusalem. Nobody was wounded; nobody was slain. So frequently God not only blesses us by the favour given, but by the way in which the gift is sent: he saves us from pains which any other method would have involved. The Lord often spares us the humiliation of being dependent upon a person who would have made his patronage bitter to us. If we had received the blessing through some great one, he might have crowed over us all the rest of his life. I like that bit in Abraham's life when the king of Sodom offered him the property which he had captured. Abraham had a right to it, for he had taken it in war; but he said, "I will not take from a thread to a shoe-latchet, lest thou shouldest say, I have made Abram rich." No, no; the servant of the Lord would not have a king talk as if he had been the maker of the Lord's own servant. God himself will so help you, so bless you, so carry you through, that you shall not have to take off your hat to any king of Sodom, neither shall he be able to go up and down the city and say, "I have made Abram rich." God will put the king of Sodom away with the horses and the horsemen, and double the mercy to you by handing it out with his own hand after his own way.

I think that the Lord does this also *to encourage you in all future troubles:* he has rescued you in a way beyond means, without means, and even against means, and therefore you cannot be in a condition from which he will be unable to rescue you. If you should come to be more friendless and more feeble than you now are—what then? Are your resources within yourself or dependent upon friends? If so, you are in an evil case. But if all your supplies are in the Lord, you are no worse off than you used to be. When the Lord strips you bare of your own garments, then you can go to his wardrobe and put on the raiment which he has provided. You cannot wear God's clothes while you glory that you are wearing your own. When want has swept your table, then all the bread on it will come from your God. When the Lord has brought you down to the bare rock, then you can go no lower, and there is a chance to build a house which will stand against flood and wind. Be reliant upon him who can work by means, but can equally well work without means whenever it seemeth good in his sight! In such confidence you will find security against all ill weathers. The Lord changes not, and therefore you shall not be consumed.

III. My time is done, or else I was going to say, thirdly, THERE IS A GOSPEL IN THIS TEXT for those here present. I can only hint at this in a few words.

The first gospel is that *salvation is possible in every case.* Notice, "I will save them." What can stand against a divine "I will"? With God nothing is impossible. If there be nothing to help him, what does it matter? He does not need help. He expressly abjures the aid of a creature when he says, "I will not save them by bow, nor by sword, nor by battle, by horses, nor by horsemen." My dear hearer, whoever you may be, there is hope in your case : if God saves, then you can be saved. If you had to save yourself, you would not be saved ; but as there is nothing wanted of you, but God worketh salvation with his own right hand, your case is hopeful. How clear is this ! And how bright with comfort !

Next, *salvation is to be sought of God alone.* Do not go wandering about to the second cause. Go straight to the Lord himself, and go at once. Straightforward is the best running in the world. Go straightforward to your God, your Saviour. Let there be no waiting for tears, feelings, repentance, sanctification, or anything else ; but arise at once, and go to your God, and for Christ's sake plead with him to have mercy upon you at this moment. As salvation does not necessarily come through the outward means, if I address any here who have neglected the outward means, let them come away to God at once, though they have neglected his courts, profaned his day, and despised his ministers. You came in here with no idea of worshipping God, but only just to see the place, and what the preacher is like. Never mind, look to the Lord Jesus Christ straight away ! With these eyes that are so blinded, look ! If you cannot see, it may be that in your obedient attempt to look, the Lord will give you sight. He does not command you to *see*, but he does command you to *look* to him and be saved : so that, if you turn your eyes towards Jesus, though they be sightless eyeballs, he will make them see. If you will trust in Christ you may cast your guilty soul on him at this moment. Why should you not do so ? Then for you the rain will be over and gone, and you will see the bright light in the clouds. Instead of the dark and dismal winter of doubt, you shall have a summer-time of hope and comfort. These dreary weeks of cold despair shall give place to a season in which heaven and earth shall blend in your experience in a joy unspeakable. The Lord grant it, for Jesus Christ's sake ! Amen.

Christ's Testimony Received

"He that hath received his testimony hath set to his seal that God is true."—John iii. 33.

In opening this discourse, I would call your attention to the different statistics given by John's disciples, and by John himself. In the twenty-sixth verse, the disciples say, "All men come to him": that is their judgment of how the ministry of Jesus was succeeding. John, in the thirty-second verse, said, "And no man receiveth his testimony." If we view them as both correct, then the disciples looked at outward appearances; and in that view the cause of Jesus seemed to be prospering to an overwhelming degree: "All men come to him." But John looked below the surface, at the true spiritual results; and his verdict was, "And no man receiveth his testimony." Be very doubtful of statistics: they depend very much upon the person compiling them. Some, with sanguine spirit, say everything that is delightful and encouraging; others, with more serious, and with perhaps more severe judgment, say much that is depressing.

I am inclined to take both these opinions with a grain of salt, each one was intended for truth, but neither of them was exact. We often hear persons say that there are crowds attending such a ministry, the people block up the gangways, they fill every seat, and the preacher is very useful, for "all men come to him." This may be true; and yet there may be few conversions, and little spiritual result; so that another may as truly say, "No man receiveth his testimony." Ah, dear friends, we can never be satisfied with a numerous congregation; we want souls to receive the testimony of Christ! Even though we may thank God that all sorts and conditions of men lend willing ears to our teaching, yet one note sounds the knell of our joy: if we hear it said, "No man receiveth his testimony," we are sad at heart.

Forgetting what the disciples reported, let us now look at what John said, "No man receiveth his testimony." He did not mean literally that no one received the truth, for his next word was, "He that hath received his testimony." He meant that *comparatively* none received it. Compared with the crowds who came to him, compared with the nation of Israel, compared with the human race, those who received Christ's testimony were so few that his sadness made him call them none. John, though he went a little below the mark, was not far from the truth when he said, "No man receiveth his testimony." In these profound and wordy days this is called the "pessimist" view of things. However, if it was not precisely the truth, it was mournfully near it. To-day, Christ is preached, and many will come to hear about him; but, alas, few receive the gospel into their hearts! Go through these crowded streets, and mark how few receive the sacred testimony. Go into our provincial towns and country villages, and note how few receive the truth as it is in Jesus. When you look at the denominational rolls at the end of the year, what small additions have been made! I think one section of the church reports one addition for the year. If any community reports as high as three or four per cent., people think wonders are accomplished. The world can never be converted at the rate at which we are now going on, for the increase of population is greater than the increase of the churches. We are relatively further back than we were. There are more Christians; but there are fewer Christians in proportion to the population. There is much reason for crying earnestly to God to work more mightily upon the hearts of men.

How glad was John to think that some had received Christ's testimony! How hungry he was that there should be more! In what earnest tones does he set forth his Lord's claims in the verses around our text! He would have men go beyond himself, and find Christ, and receive his testimony.

This is how the case stands. Men had wandered far from God; God desired that men should come back to him; and therefore he sent a witness to men to tell them of his kindly feelings towards them, and to show in his own person, teaching, life, and death how really and truly God desired that men should be at peace with him. The only-begotten Son was born into our world, and took our nature, that he might be a witness to the people of the character of God towards us; that we, knowing how God felt, might be led to cry, "Come, and let us return unto the Lord." He would have us touched with tender relentings when we discover the greatness of the love and mercy of God towards us, by seeing him seeking and saving the lost in the person of his only-begotten Son.

Of that subject I am going to speak this morning, keeping as closely as I can to the text, and crying to the Holy Spirit for aid.

First, *observe the testifier* carefully. Look at him, and see who it is that has come to reveal the Father unto us. Secondly, *hearken to his testimony*. What is it? Know it, and believe it. Thirdly, *note the rejecters:* "No man receiveth his testimony." How sad is the fact! Then, coming closer still to the text, *commune with those who do receive his heaven-given testimony*. Of these it is said that they have set to their seal that God is true.

I. First, let us OBSERVE THE TESTIFIER. Jesus, our Lord, as a witness, is so wrapped up with the testimony which he bears, that you have to know him before you can understand his witness: in fact, to receive *him* is the same thing as to receive his testimony. If we have received Christ as what he is, we have received the testimony which he came to bear.

Who is this testifier? this witness? We answer that, according to the context, it is "*he that cometh from above.*" To save us, there has not come to us a man whose origin was at his birth, but one who existed long before, and descended from above. It is true that Jesus was born at Bethlehem; but it is equally true that he had a pre-existence from before all worlds. The Word was from the beginning with God; "without him was not anything made that was made." He was God as truly before he became man as ever he was after-wards. He that has come to save us has, in the highest sense, come from above. Let this kindle hope in the sinner's mind, and let it draw forth faith in the divine ambassador. One has come from the highest heavens to lift those up, who, apart from him, must have sunk into the lowest hell. Nearly nineteen hundred years have passed since he came and trod the roughest ways of this world, and lived, and sorrowed, and suffered here below. From the hills of heaven he came to this land of sin, that he might lift us up, and give us a divine inheritance.

He was one of the very highest character. Observe: "He that cometh from above is above all: he that is of the earth is earthly, and speaketh of the earth: he that cometh from heaven is above all." All other messengers that God has sent have had much earthliness about them; and, assuredly, we who are now his messengers, have much of it. "We have this treasure in earthen vessels;" but there was nothing in our Lord Jesus that could debase the messenger. He was pure, perfect, heavenly; and though he bore our nature, yet he shared not our sinfulness; and though he spoke in our tongue, and brought down the mysteries of heaven to our comprehension, yet still he spoke them in a heavenly style—a style to which a mere man could never have reached. Moses wrote as a man, and the Spirit of God only revealed truth measurably by him; but our Lord Jesus Christ was full of grace and truth, and he spoke with a manhood united to Godhead, having the Spirit without measure. In all Jesus said there was a fulness, a power, a reality, which mere men were not capable of containing. He was above all; and others derived their authority from him, "for the testimony of Jesus is the spirit of prophecy." Will you not listen to one so supreme? "God, who at sundry times and in divers manners spake in time past unto the fathers by the prophets, hath in these last days spoken unto us by his Son;" surely it shall go ill with him that refuseth such a messenger.

As he was above all in character, *so was he above all in rank.* None can be compared with him for dignity: the angels may be peers of the heavenly realm, but he is the Crown Prince, of the Blood-royal of eternity. He is God over all, before whom cherubim and seraphim veil their faces. He deigned to become subject to parents, but he was, none the less, above all, Lord, Ruler, Head over all things. Though he stooped to seek and save the lost, he was still higher than the highest: though he laid his glory by, that he might wash his disciples' feet; yea, and wash our sins away in his own blood; yet he was still Master and Lord. " See that ye refuse not him that speaketh. For if they escaped not who refused him that spake on earth, much more shall not we escape, if we turn away from him that speaketh from heaven." I cannot too highly speak of the glory and honour and majesty which belong to our Emmanuel. If I had the tongues of men and of angels, I could not sufficiently extol him. He is the First-born of every creature, yea, the Creator himself. King of kings, and Lord of lords is he ; and it is through so glorious a person as this that God hath sent to us a message of peace. Our ambassador is of a rank above all ranks, that the Lord may show how highly he esteems his chosen of the race of man. We are greatly honoured by dealing with so august a messenger. Come, ye willing hearts, and gladly receive the testimony of him who is above all !

We are further told by John a very important fact, which ought to weigh with every thoughtful mind. *The testimony of Jesus is personal testimony* : " what he hath seen and heard, that he testifieth." The prophets received their prophecies from the Holy Spirit, who spake to them of things which they had not seen. Sometimes they did not even understand what they wrote ; they did not see those things of which they wrote, for it is written that " many prophets and kings have desired to see those things, but have not seen them." These things even angels desired to look into, but they were too mysterious for them. Our Lord Jesus Christ knows heavenly things of his own proper knowledge, for he has ever dwelt in the bosom of the Father. He knows the mind of God, for he is God. The secret intent and purpose of the Most High God are with his Son Jesus. All that he reveals to men of the mercy of God he has himself seen and heard. He was an eye and ear witness of the mind and will of Jehovah. Christ's teaching is not second-hand : " No man knoweth the Father, save the Son." Who taught him wisdom ? Whence hath this Man knowledge ? From his own self, from his own eternal experience, as dwelling with God before all worlds, he speaks to us. Do you want a better messenger, my hearers ? How can the Lord serve you better than by sending one who knows what he declares—knows it by having heard, and seen, and handled it ? With the God who made the heavens and fashioned the earth he ever dwelt, as one brought up with him, and he was daily his delight. The Lord God has sent as ambassador to you one whom he " possessed in the beginning of his way, before his works of old." What more can you desire ?

And then, further, the Baptist goes on to tell us that *the testimony of Jesus is identical with the words of God himself.* " He that hath received his testimony hath set to his seal that *Christ* is true." Do you see, I am reading amiss ? The Scripture saith, " that *God* is true." The testimony of Jesus and the testimony of God are one ; and when you believe Christ Jesus, you believe God. Further on we read, " for he whom God hath sent speaketh the words of God : for God giveth not the Spirit by measure unto him." If you deny what Christ says, you make God a liar ; for you have not believed his testimony concerning his Son. So fully is the witness of Jesus backed up and supported by the words of God, so fully does Jesus represent the purpose and the mind of the Father, that to doubt him is to doubt the Eternal God. Now, if you have a plan of salvation put before you by God's messenger—which is most assuredly the very mind of God himself—will you reject it? Will you fly in the face of God by rejecting salvation, which comes stamped in every letter of it with divine authority? I pray you, my hearers, if you have not yet believed in Jesus, remain no longer in unbelief of him, for it is unbelief of the Lord God, unbelief of the Triune Jehovah, who made you, and who keeps the breath in your nostrils. See what a messenger we have, then, who speaks not his own words, but the words of him that sent him. Those words are full of grace and truth; for they are full of God.

Read a little further on, in the next verse, and you will see that this messenger whom God hath sent is *one in high esteem with God.* "The Father loveth the Son." To show his great love of him, he "hath given all things into his hand." You have not now to deal with God out of Christ, for all things are now put under the mediatorial government of the Son of God. Christ Jesus, the Mediator between God and men, hath all things in his power: the government is upon his shoulder. It has pleased the Father to put all things under the man Christ Jesus:

> "Life, death, and hell, and worlds unknown
> Hang on his sacred will."

Jesus is absolute Master of all things; angels fly, and devils tremble, at his nod, and all the wheels of Providence revolve in perfect order according to his will. If you listen to his testimony of grace, remember that he has all power to back it up, and make it true to you. "He is able to save to the uttermost." All power is given unto him in heaven and in earth. God hath put all things under his feet: and he who is thus the Lord of all, has come to treat with you concerning reconciliation. Turn not on your heel, ye busy men; say not that you have no time to attend to him! Ye must attend to One whose kingdom ruleth over all. Dare you treat him with indifference? Will not the awe of his majesty constrain you to hearken to his voice?

Once more only. Concerning this testifier, we learn that *he is the Lord and Giver of life,* and if we will but accept his testimony we shall live thereby. He hath life in himself, and he has power to quicken whomsoever he will. "He that believeth on the Son hath everlasting life." And, to make the matter still more pressing, the word of warning is added, "He that believeth not the Son shall not see life; but the wrath of God abideth on him." God can never be pleased with a person who gives the lie to his own Son. He has, in boundless pity, sent his Son, his only-begotten Son, to live and die, that men might be saved; how shall he endure to see him rejected? "God so loved the world, that he gave his only-begotten Son, that whosoever believeth in him should not perish, but have everlasting life." And if this Son of his love be refused, if the guilty insult the Father by rejecting the Son, what can remain but righteous wrath? If a deed of mercy, unspeakable, immeasurable, comes to be despised by you, then the anger must abide upon you. There is no hope for those who refuse Jesus. Flatter not yourselves that there is another way of escape, in some future state; for if there could have been another way, God would not have given up his Son to shame, suffering, and death. Faith in Jesus is the only door of hope; shut that upon yourselves, and you shut yourselves in outer darkness, in helpless, hopeless misery. What can help you if the wrath of God abideth on you? This must mean a misery unspeakable, without the slightest alleviation. O my dear hearers, I wish I had the power to set forth my Lord as the witness! As I cannot do this as I would, I commend to you the passage of Scripture itself. The sentences are short, sharp, crisp, clear, and they show you who he is whom God hath sent on the great errand of divine love. Refuse him not, I implore you.

II. Secondly, HEARKEN TO HIS TESTIMONY. What is the testimony of Jesus? What has the Christ to tell us concerning God? I will only use the three chapters which precede my text, and I shall gather enough from them to give a fair outline of what Jesus tells us of the Father, and his willingness to forgive and save.

First, he tells us, *God has provided an atonement*. Look at the twenty-ninth verse of the first chapter, where John says, "Behold the Lamb of God, which taketh away the sin of the world." The very fact that the Son of God came here as man to suffer for our sin, proves that God has provided a great and all-sufficient sacrifice. God could not deal with a sinful world, it was too defiled with sin for him to look upon it; but that sin of the world which prevented a holy God from dealing with a condemned race, has been taken away by Jesus, so that now the Lord can visit man, and favour him with the gospel of peace, and the work of salvation. This was needful before a single individual could be saved. "God was in Christ, reconciling the world unto himself." The death of Jesus has enabled God to treat with men. Oh, hear ye this! There is a sacrifice for sin! My hearers, believe it, and make much if it. The blood of Jesus Christ his Son cleanseth us from all sin. Jesus has died; and in that death he has finished transgression, made an end of sin, and brought in everlasting righteousness. All believers are forgiven through his death. God is willing that you, believing in his dear Son, should be so forgiven as to be washed whiter than snow. That is Christ's testimony to you; and he that receiveth it hath set to his seal that God is true.

The next testimony of Jesus is that *the Lord has made a way of access between man and God*. See you the fifty-first verse of the first chapter. He said to Nathanael, "Verily, verily, I say unto you, hereafter ye shall see heaven open, and the angels of God ascending and descending upon the Son of man." Jacob's ladder is not now before you as a dream, but as a reality. The Son of man, the Incarnate God, God in Christ Jesus, is the way by which there can be commerce between man and God. We can go up to God, and the angels of God, loaded with blessings, can come down to men. The gulf is bridged: a glorious stairway has been made across the dread abyss which separated guilty man from his offended God. Jesus Christ himself, in his own person, is that ladder, and he bears witness thereof to you. Sin is put away, and distance is removed.

What is the next part of his testimony? You will find it in the third chapter: *God is only to be approached in a spiritual way*. To come to God, "ye must be born again." That which is born of flesh is flesh, and cannot commune with God, who is a spirit. That which is born of the Spirit is spirit, and can commune with the holy God, and understand spiritual things. My hearers, there is no coming to God by a priest of human consecration, no coming by outward ritual, form, and ceremony: "God is a Spirit: and they that worship him must worship him in spirit and in truth." You must have a spiritual nature, that the Spirit of God may commune with you. Only by a spiritual nature can you have intercourse with the great Invisible. Your spirit can be in fellowship with God, the mighty Spirit; but what can you do till a spirit is created in you? This was our Lord's testimony to Nathanael; and I suppose that, by some means, John the Baptist had heard of it; but whether he had or had not does not matter to my purpose at this time; it is certainly a part of the testimony of Jesus.

Furthermore, our Lord bore testimony to the great fact that *God gives salvation to all believers in Jesus,* and to make that very plain, he puts it thus—"As Moses lifted up the serpent in the wilderness, even so must the Son of man be lifted up: that whosoever believeth in him should not perish, but have eternal life." You know the type. Bitten by the fiery serpents, the people looked to the brazen serpent, and they were healed. Now, bitten by sin, you look to him, who was made sin for us; and, looking to him, your guilt passes away, and the poison of your sinfulness meets its antidote. We look to Jesus and live. Our Lord bore witness to this with his own lips, and then by the lips of his apostles. He still cries, "Look unto me, and be ye saved, all the ends of the earth." Yes, there is life in a look at the Crucified One. Believing is receiving. Accept Christ, whom God sends as a messenger to you, and in accepting him you shall be saved.

Jesus also testified plainly that *from all who believe in him the Lord has removed condemnation.* It is written, "He that believeth on him is not condemned." He that believeth is justified, and "being justified by faith, we have peace with God." Guilty and condemned as you may be at this hour, if you accept the Son of God to stand for you, you are not condemned. "There is therefore now no condemnation to them which are in Christ Jesus." Though your sins be as scarlet, they shall be as white as snow. Though by nature robed in rags, the Lord saith, "Take away the filthy garments from him." Your glorious challenge is, "Who shall lay anything to the charge of God's elect?" "Who is he that condemneth? It is Christ that died." Oh! this message of mercy from Jesus, is it not full and blessed? If I had the time, I should like to have enlarged much upon the testimony of God in Christ Jesus; but here it means just this, that you, being guilty and condemned, can be justly forgiven, through the sacrifice of Jesus. You may be beloved of God because of his love to Jesus; and delivered from all the evil results of sin because of the death of the Well-beloved. You can be saved; yea, if you now believe in Christ Jesus, you are saved. All heavenly privileges are yours now, where you now sit, and shall be yours world without end. Glory be to God!

III. With great heaviness we have now to NOTICE THE REJECTERS: —"No man receiveth his testimony." You would have thought that he moment this testimony was delivered to the world every man would have hastened to hear it, and would have believed it with joyful readiness: but, alas, the very reverse happened! If I went to fish with such bait as this, I should expect to have a sea full of fish rushing towards me; but it was not so. Men, as a rule, will not accept this heavenly salvation: no man will receive it except moved by God the Holy Ghost. Why is this?

In the case of many, *it is because they are earthly;* the message and the messenger are too heavenly for them. They are earth-bound, and earth-buried. They are so busy; how can they consider the grand fact that God has come down to save men? They will think of that great spiritual truth one of these days when they have made sufficient money, and can retire, and have nothing better to do than to attend to the claims of God. God is second-rate, nay, seventh-rate in their esteem. They are really so occupied, and their thoughts are so taken up with daily cares of this life, that God's grace must wait their convenience. I fear they will never be startled into thought until it is said of each one of them, "In hell he lift up his eyes, being in torments." The rich man had kept his eyes downward upon his sumptuous faring, and had never looked up to heavenly things; but the realities of eternity awakened him. O God, grant that none of my hearers may keep their eyes down until they lift them up in hell!

Some rejecters of the Word of our Lord, I have no doubt, were *too learned to believe in anything so simple* as the statement that God was among them in human form, to live and die for men. Though this is in very truth the sublimest of all mysteries, yet human pride counts it a small matter: it is to the Jews a stumbling-block, and to the Greeks foolishness. Men know so much that they will not know God. I am struck every day, when reviewing books of the present period, with how wise fools are nowadays. Pardon me; I will put it differently, and say—how foolish the wise are nowadays. I mean the same thing, whichever way I say it. They get a hold of the tail of a dead thing, and they shout like men that find great spoil. Here is a great discovery —a discovery of nothing! At one time they find Deuteronomy to be a fraud; next there are two Isaiahs; anon, the book of Ruth was written far down in the centuries after the exile; Jonah is a myth, Esther is a romance, and so forth. Their criticisms are all false, as others of the same breed soon show. They are always finding some dead cat or other, and setting it out on the table, where the children's bread ought to be. What mighty discoveries of mares' nests we have lived to see! Men of this nature will not receive the witness of Jesus: it is a pity that they should: he is honoured by their rejection. You can scarcely read a book nowadays, but you come across a bit of rotten stuff, the fondly-cherished nonsense of some writer who has a taste for that which is far gone in decay. They will not believe God. **How can** they while they receive honour one of another, as learned critics? **It** is to-day as it was in our Lord's time, "not many wise men after the flesh are called." Still have we to ask, "Where is the wise? where is the scribe? where is the disputer of this world?" Those who glory in fleshly wisdom cannot receive the testimony of the carpenter's Son—

a testimony so plain that the poor and illiterate can understand it, and enter into eternal life thereby. I hope this will not be the case with any of the more cultured among you. Be willing to take Christ's yoke upon you, and learn of him.

Certain people did not receive the testimony of Jesus because they were too proud. Pedigree and privilege kept many away. Read this verse in the first chapter:—"He came unto his own, and his own received him not." Why? Because they thought they were God's own already. Did they not wear a text of Scripture between their eyes? Had they not broad fringes of blue to their dress? Did they not tithe mint, and anise, and cummin, and other pennyworths of herbs? Did they not fast thrice in the week, and so on? What did they want with Jesus? Those who professed to belong to God, and cried, "The temple of the Lord, the temple of the Lord are we," were too good to accept a Saviour, too near to heaven to need a messenger from God.

The real reason for rejecting the testimony of Jesus was this—*they were too evil to receive it.* Read verse 19: "Light is come into the world, and men loved darkness rather than light, because their deeds were evil. For every one that doeth evil hateth the light, neither cometh to the light, lest his deeds should be reproved." Ah, my unbelieving hearers, if you were better men, you would more readily accept the light of Christ! If men were not such sinners as they are, they would come to him to learn the way of the Lord. Alas! the depth of man's guilt has hardened his heart, and darkened his perceptions, and made him prefer darkness to light. Men do not see that they need deliverance; they hear music in the rattle of their chains. May the Spirit of God come, and convince men of sin; and when they are once convinced of it, and foresee their doom, they will change their minds towards the Saviour, and be willing to hear the message of divine grace. May God, of his boundless grace, save every man and woman and child to whom this sermon shall come! I am greatly pleased to see so many of you present on such a wet and stormy day as this: I hope the Lord means to bless you now that you are here. I remember going to the house of God one morning when there were only a few persons able to reach the place, there being a heavy snow-storm at the time. That morning I found the Saviour by looking to him upon the cross; and now I look with great interest upon services which are held in rough weather. I hope that those who have had the determination to come are more than common hearers; I trust that they have hearts that the Lord God has touched. I hope you have come hither with a desire to find salvation, and if so, may you find it in the Lord Jesus at once! O Lord, grant it, I beseech thee!

All the while, remember, these rejecters of Christ *were under the wrath of God.* What a terrible condition! I will not dwell upon the awful fact; but let a man only know the meaning of these words, and he will tremble in his seat—"He that believeth not the Son shall not see life; but the wrath of God abideth on him." O souls, how can you bear it?

IV. We will conclude by speaking upon the fourth point. Let

US COMMUNE WITH THOSE WHO RECEIVE CHRIST'S TESTIMONY. The text says, "He that hath received his testimony hath set to his seal that God is true." To receive is, in still plainer Saxon, "*to take in.*" There is here the idea of retaining as well as receiving. We take in the testimony of Jesus that it may abide in us. We hear what Jesus says, and we answer to it, "Lord, I believe." Our word is, "Master, say on. Whatever thou sayest, I believe." We take in all that Jesus witnesses, and we hold to it. We believe, and we keep on believing. We come to Jesus, and we are always coming to him. Some people begin with believing in Jesus, and then turn aside to believe in their own feelings; but you must not do so. You must believe, and keep right on believing. The just shall live by faith. We receive Christ, and keep on receiving him. "He that receiveth his testimony." Do you refuse anything to which Jesus witnesses? This is evil. Receive his testimony with unquestioning faith. Some men will believe any monstrous assertion of scientists, or spiritualists, or rationalists; but they cannot believe the plain witness of the Lord Jesus Christ. The man who takes in the teaching of Jesus, and keeps to it, he is the blessed man.

He takes in the testimony of Jesus for himself, and receives it as his own possession. That Jesus saves from sin is true; that he saves *me* from sin is a more personal truth. Christ will save those who believe. This is good. But "I believe, and therefore I am saved," is better. Personal appropriation is the best receiving. Accept the truth of Jesus for your own soul; seize it by the grip of a personal faith, and then you have it. You have seen a boy with a burning-glass—he concentrates all the rays of the sun so as to produce a burning; even so, by faith, concentrate the testimony of Jesus upon your own case, and you will soon feel a wonderful power working in your soul. He that receives the testimony of Jesus makes it his own, feeds on it, and is saved thereby.

Receivers of Christ's testimony allow nothing to make them doubt what he has said. When the believer is down in the dumps, and is passing through a dark time, he says, "What Jesus has said is true for all this. He has told me that, if I believe in him, I have eternal life, and I have it, however gloomy things may appear. I have a sluggish liver, and it makes me feel low and miserable; but I have eternal life. My wife is sickening to death, and I have buried child after child, and lost friend after friend; but I have eternal life. God's waves and billows go over me, but I have eternal life; for he says it, and I cannot doubt him." It is a grand thing to have your confidence outside yourself; it is glorious to have it all in Christ. As long as you keep your confidence in your own self, it will be a very poor stay for you. There is a ship at sea, and a foolish landsman feels very confident of the safety of the vessel because they have a big anchor on board. My dear man, what is the good of that anchor while it is on board? It would rather tend to sink the ship by its weight than to be of service to it. "Oh," says he, "but it is one of the best Admiralty anchors, and we are safe while that is on board!" O simple soul, an anchor is of no use while you can see it! Drop it down into the deep sea, out of sight, and then it will be of service.

Hear the chain run out! Now the anchor is far down, it grips, and holds the vessel. You must fix your confidence within the veil. Your anchorage of hope must be where mortal eyes can never see. Our rest lies in simply believing the word of the Lord Jesus. I believe it, though I do not feel it. I believe it, though I cannot argue the matter out logically. I believe it, because God says it to me through his great witness, the Lord Jesus Christ.

The foregoing will enable you to see the truth of the statement, "He that hath received his testimony *hath set to his seal that God is true.*" In the olden time men did not often write their names, because they could not write at all. Even kings set their seals, because they could not give a signature. To this day, how often does it happen to me, as a trustee to a chapel or a school, to have a paper laid before me, and I not only sign my name, but I put my finger on that red wafer, which represents my seal, and I say, "This is my act and deed"! When you believe in Jesus, you have set your seal to the testimony of Jesus, which is the revelation of the Lord. You have certified that you believe in God as true. What does that mean? It means not only that he has kept his promise as made to the fathers in the Old Testament, and will keep it in Christ Jesus; but it means also, that to you *God is real.* By faith in Jesus you have come to know the reality of God. Before, you talked about an unknown God, but now you know him, and declare your faith in his reality and fidelity. Now you perceive substance, and not shadow. Now you see mystery, but not myth. God is truth, and all that Jesus said of him is truth. He says, "He that believeth on the Son hath everlasting life"; and you find that God is true, for you live in newness of life. Jesus says, "He that believeth on him is not condemned"; and you know it is so, for you enjoy a sense of pardoned sin. You have sealed the testimony of God by resting your own soul upon it. It seems a very joyful thing to me that I should be allowed to be a witness to the truth of God. I feel honoured by being allowed to subscribe my name to the testimony of Jesus. Can you not do the same? Remember what it involves. You doubting Christians, what are you doing? You have already put your hand and seal to the promise of God, and are you going to contradict your own signature and seal? When you first believed in Jesus, you set to your seal that God is true; and now, because you have met with a little trouble, are you going to retract your witness? Do you fear that the Lord will not help you, and save you? What are we to understand by that seal of yours? Is God, after all, untrue, or unreal? You know better. Shame on you for contradicting yourself! Remember, when you make God a liar, you make yourself a liar, for you have already set your hand and seal to it that God is true; and seals and handwritings remain. You accepted the real Saviour for your real sin, and you believed in the real death of Christ for you: are you going to run back? Will you doubt your Lord after this? God grant you may not; but, on the contrary, may you go on confirming the testimony of Jesus, and setting it to your seal again and again that God is true! Give glory to God by believing that what he has promised he is able also to perform. Never stagger at the promise through unbelief. All the promises of

God are yea and amen in Christ Jesus, to the glory of God by us; wherefore, we set to our seal that God is true.

I have done, when I have said just this. Avoid, dear hearers, anxiously, the double sin of unbelief. If you do not believe Jesus, you do not believe God. If you reject his Son, you reject himself. If you give the lie to the teaching of Christ, you give the lie to God. Flee from this deadly sin.

Note well the simple matter upon which eternal life depends. "He that believeth on the Son hath everlasting life." He has it *now;* it is in his heart now; and it is not for a time, for it is everlasting life. Note that, as soon as a man believes God, he sets to his seal that God is true, and then away flies all suspicion of his God. Our sins are largely caused by our mistrust of God. You think that God denies you something that would be good for you, and therefore you go and take it. You suspect God of being so cruel as to command you to do that which is to your injury, and so you refuse to obey him. Now if you believe that God is true, you will henceforth give up what he bids you give up, because you feel that it is well to do so; and you will act as he bids you, because you are sure his command is wise and good. Between you and God there will be henceforth a holy confidence; and what will that lead to? It will lead to holiness of life, and earnest seeking to please God, in whom you unreservedly believe. You will love him with all your heart, and with all your soul, now that confidence is created. See what a change faith makes! Have you never heard of a servant who believed hard things of her mistress? She thought her a tyrant, and resolved that she would do nothing to please her. When she did her work, she did it very badly, and thought it was quite good enough for such a creature as her mistress. But she heard something about her which entirely changed her opinion. Instead of thinking her a demon, she judged her to be little less than an angel. It might have seemed a small matter, but it was not so. She did her work zealously and gladly now that her suspicions were ended. Faith in her mistress affected her whole life. So is it in spiritual things. Faith in Christ Jesus is the fountain of obedience, the ensign of a change of heart. God grant it to you all! Amen.

The Simplicity and Sublimity
of Salvation

"He came unto his own, and his own received him not. But as many as received him, to them gave he power to become the sons of God, even to them that believe on his name: Which were born, not of blood, nor of the will of the flesh, nor of the will of man, but of God."—John i. 11—13.

EVERYTHING here is simple; everything is sublime. Here is that simple gospel, by which the most ignorant may be saved. Here are profundities, in which the best-instructed may find themselves beyond their depth. Here are those everlasting hills of divine truth which man cannot climb; yet here is that plain path in which the wayfaring man, though a fool, need not err, nor lose his way. I always feel that I have no time to spare for critical and captious persons. If they will not believe, neither shall they be established. They must take the consequences of their unbelief. But I can spare all day and all night for an anxious enquirer, for one who is blinded by the very blaze of the heavenly light that shines upon him, and who seems to lose his way by reason of the very plainness of the road that lies before him. In this most simple text are some of the deep things of God, and there are souls here that are puzzled by what are simplicities to some of us; and my one aim shall be, so to handle this text as to help and encourage and cheer some who would fain touch the hem of the Master's garment, but cannot for the press of many difficulties and grave questions which rise before their minds.

Let us go to the text at once, and notice, first, *a matter which is very simple:* "As many as received him . . . . even to them that believe on his name"; secondly, *a matter which is very delightful:* "to them gave he power to become the sons of God"; and thirdly, *a matter which is very mysterious:* "Which were born, not of blood, nor of the will of the flesh, nor of the will of man, but of God."

I. Here is, first, A MATTER WHICH IS VERY SIMPLE; receiving Christ, and believing on his name. Oh, that many here may be able to say,

"Yes, I understand that simple matter. That is the way in which I found eternal life"!

The simple matter of which John here speaks is receiving Christ, or, in other words, believing on his name.

Receiving Christ is *a distinctive act*. "He came unto his own, and his own received him not." The very people you would have thought would have eagerly welcomed Christ did not do so; but here and there a man stood apart from the rest, or a woman came out from her surroundings, and each of these said, "I receive Christ as the Messiah." You will never go to heaven in a crowd. The crowd goes down the broad road to destruction; but the way which leadeth to life eternal is a narrow way; "and few there be that find it." They that go to heaven must come out one by one, and say to him that sits at the wicket-gate, "Set my name down, sir, as a pilgrim to the celestial city." They who would enter into life must fight as well as run, for it is an uphill fight all the way, and few there be that fight it out to the end, and win the crown of the victors.

Those who received Christ were different from those who did not receive him; they were as different as white is from black, or light from darkness. They took a distinct step, separated themselves from others, and came out and received him whom others would not receive. Have you taken such a step, dear friend? Can you say, "Yes, let others do as they will, as for me, Christ is all my salvation, and all my desire; and at all hazards I am quite content to be counted singular, and to stand alone; I have lifted my hand to heaven, and I cannot draw back. Whatever others may do, I say, 'Christ for me'"?

As it was a distinctive act, so it was *a personal one:* "To as many as received him." They had to receive Christ each one by his own act and deed. "Even to them that believe on his name." Believing is the distinct act of a person. I cannot believe for you any more than you can believe for me; that is clearly impossible. There can be no such thing as sponsorship in receiving Christ or in faith. If you are an unbeliever, your father and your mother may be the most eminent saints, but their faith does not overlap and cover your unbelief. You must believe for yourself. I have had even to remind some that the Holy Ghost himself cannot believe for them. He works faith in you; but you have to believe. The faith must be your own distinct mental act. Faith is the gift of God; but God does not believe for us; how could he? It is for you distinctly to believe. Come, dear hearer, have you been trying to put up with a national faith? A national faith is a mere sham. Or have you tried to think that you possess the family faith? "Oh, we are all Christians, you know!" Yes, we are all hypocrites; that is what that comes to. Unless each one is a Christian for himself, he is a Christian only in name, and that is to be a hypocrite. Oh, that we might have the certainty that we have each one laid our sins on Jesus, the spotless Lamb of God! God grant that, if we have never done so before, we may do so this very moment!

Mark, next, that, as it was a distinctive and personal act, so *it related to a Person.* I find that the text runs thus, "He came unto his own, and his own received him not. But as many as received him, to them gave he power to become the sons of God, even to them that believe on his name." That religion which leaves out the person of Christ, has left out the essential point. Thou art not saved by believing a doctrine, though it is well for thee to believe it if it be true. Thou art not saved by practising an ordinance, though thou shouldst practise it if thou art one of those to whom it belongs. Thou art not saved by any belief except this, believing on Christ's name, and receiving him. "I take in a body of divinity," says one. Do you? There is no body of divinity that I know of but Christ, who is divinity embodied. Beware of resting on a system of theology. Thou must rest on him who is the true Theology, the Word of God; on Christ, the Son of God in human flesh, living, bleeding, dying, risen, ascended, soon to come; thou must lean on him; for the promise is only to as many as receive him.

This reception of Christ *consisted in faith in him:* "As many as received him . . . . even to them that believe on his name." He was a stranger, and they took him in. He was food, and they took him in, and fed on him. He was living water, and they received him, drank him up, took him into themselves. He was light, and they received the light. He was life, and they received the life, and they lived by what they received. It is a beautiful description of faith, the act of receiving. As the empty cup receives from the flowing fountain, so do we receive Christ into our emptiness. We, being poor, and naked, and miserable, come to him, and we receive riches, and clothing, and happiness in him. Salvation comes by receiving Christ. I know what you have been trying to do; you have been trying to give Christ something. Let me caution you against a very common expression. I hear converts continually told to give their hearts to Jesus. It is quite correct, and I hope that they will do so; but your first concern must be, not what you give to Jesus, but what Jesus gives to you. You must take him from himself as his gift to you, then will you truly give your heart to him. The first act, and, indeed, the underlying act all the way along, is to receive, to imbibe, to take in Christ, and that is called believing on his name. Note that "name." It is not believing a fanciful christ; for there are many christs nowadays, as many christs as there are books, nearly; for every writer seems to make a christ of his own; but the christ that men make up will not save you. The only Christ who can save you is the Christ of God, that Christ who, in the synagogue at Nazareth, found the place where it was written, "The Spirit of the Lord is upon me, because he hath anointed me to preach the gospel to the poor; he hath sent me to heal the brokenhearted, to preach deliverance to the captives, and recovering of sight to the blind, to set at liberty them that are bruised, to preach the acceptable year of the Lord."

You are to believe on *the Christ as he is revealed in the Scriptures.* You are to take him as you find him here; not as Renan, or Strauss, or anybody else, pictures him; but as you find him here. As God reveals him, you are to believe on his name: "the Wonderful, Counsellor, the Mighty God, the Everlasting Father, the Prince of Peace"; Emmanuel, God with us; Jesus, saving from sin; Christ, anointed of the Father. You are to believe on his name, not on the Christ of Rome, nor the Christ of Canterbury, but the Christ of Jerusalem, the Christ of the eternal glory; no christ of a dreamy prophecy, with which some are defaming the true prophetic spirit of the Word, no christ of idealism, no man-made christ; but the eternal God, incarnate in human flesh, as he is here pictured by Psalmist, Prophet, Evangelist, Apostle, very God of very God, yet truly man, in your stead suffering, bearing the sin of men in his own body on the tree. It is believing in this Christ that will effectually save your soul. To believe is to trust. Prove that you believe in Christ by risking everything upon him.

> "Upon a life I did not live,
> Upon a death I did not die,
> I risk my whole eternity."

On him who lived for me, and died for me, and rose again for me, and has gone into heaven for me; on him I throw the whole weight of past, present, and future, and every interest that belongs to my soul, for time and for eternity.

This is a very simple matter, and I have noticed a great many sneers at this simple faith, and a great many depreciatory remarks concerning it; but, let me tell you, there is nothing like it under heaven. Possessing this faith will prove you to be a son of God; nothing short of it ever will. "To as many as received him, to them gave he power to become the sons of God;" and he has given that power to nobody else. This will prove you to be absolved, forgiven. "There is, therefore, now no condemnation to them which are in Christ Jesus;" but if thou hast no faith in Christ Jesus, the wrath of God abideth on thee. Because thou hast not believed on the Son of God, thou art condemned already. One grain of this faith is worth more than a diamond the size of the world; yea, though thou shouldst thread such jewels together, as many as the stars of heaven for number, they would be worth nothing compared with the smallest atom of faith in Jesus Christ, the eternal Son of God.

But whence comes this wonderful power of faith? Not from the faith, but from him on whom it leans. What power Christ has! The power of his manhood suffering, the power of his Godhead bowing on the cross, the power of the God-man, the Mediator, surrendering himself as the great sacrifice for sin; why, he who toucheth this, hath touched the springs of omnipotence! He who comes, by faith, into contact with Christ, has come into contact with boundless love, and power, and mercy, and grace. I marvel not at anything that faith brings when it deals with Christ. Thou hast a little key, a little rusty key, and thou sayest, "By the use of this key I can get all the gold that I want." Yes, but where is the box to which you go for the gold? When you show me, and I see that it is a great chamber filled full of gold and silver, I can understand how your little key can enrich you when it opens the door into such a treasury. If faith be the key which unlocks the fulness of God, "for it pleased the Father that in him should all fulness dwell," then I can understand why faith brings such boundless blessings to him who hath it. Salvation is a very simple business. God help us to look at it simply, and practically, and to receive Christ, and believe on his name!

II. Now, secondly, here is A MATTER WHICH IS VERY DELIGHTFUL: "To them gave he power to become the sons of God."

If I had a week in which to preach from this text, I think that I should be able to get through the first head; but at this time I can only throw out just a few hints. Look at the great and delightful blessing which comes to us by our faith in Christ. We give Christ our faith, and he gives us power to become sons of God, the authority, liberty, privilege, right,—something more than mere strength or force—to be sons of God.

When we believe in Jesus, he indicates to us *the Great Father's willingness to let us be his sons*. We who were prodigals, far away from him, perceive that, when we receive Christ, the Father, who gave us Christ, is willing to take us to be his sons. He would not have yielded up his Only-begotten if he had not willed to take us into his family.

When we believe in Jesus, *he bestows on us the status of sons*. We were slaves before; now we are sons. We were strangers, aliens, enemies; any and every word that means an evil thing might have been applied to us; but when we laid hold on Christ, we were regarded as the sons of God. As a man in Rome, when he was adopted by some great citizen, and publicly acknowledged in the forum as being henceforth that man's son, was really regarded as such, so, as soon as we believe in Jesus, we get the status of sons. "Beloved, now are we the sons of God."

Then Christ does something more for us. *He gives us grace to feel our sonship*. As we sang just now,—

> "My faith shall 'Abba, Father,' cry,
> And thou the kindred own."

God owns us as his children, and we own him as our Father; and henceforth, "Our Father, which art in heaven," is no meaningless expression, but it comes welling up from the depths of our heart.

Having given us grace to feel sonship, *Christ gives us the nature of our Father*. He gives us "power to become the sons of God." We get more and more like God in righteousness and true holiness. By his divine Spirit, shed abroad in our hearts, we become more and more the children of our Father who is in heaven, who doeth good to the undeserving and the unthankful, and whose heart overflows with love even to those who love not him.

When this nature of sons shall be fully developed, *Christ will bestow his glory upon us*. We shall be in heaven, not in the rear rank, as servants, but nearest to the eternal throne. Unto the angels he has never said, "Ye are my sons"; but he has called us sons, poor creatures of the dust, who believe in Jesus; and we shall have all the honour, and joy, and privilege, and delight that belong to princes of the blood royal of heaven, members of the imperial house of God, in that day when the King shall manifest himself in his own palace.

Some of us could draw parallels, about being made sons, from our own lives. You were once a very tiny child; but you were a son then as much as you are now. So is it with you who have only just begun to believe in Christ; he has given you authority and right to become the sons of God. Very early in our life, our father went down to the registrar's office, and wrote our name in the roll as his sons. We do not recollect that, it is so long ago; but he did it, and he also wrote our names in the family Bible, even as our Father who is in heaven has enrolled our names in the Lamb's Book of Life. You recollect that, as a child, you did not go in the kitchen, to dine with the servants; but you took your seat at the table. It was a very little chair in which you first sat at the table; but as you grew bigger, you always went to the table, because you were a son. The servants in the house were much bigger than you, and they could do a great many things that you could not do, and your father paid them wages. He never paid you any; they were not his sons, but you were. If they had put on your clothes, they would not have been his sons. You had privileges that they had not. I remember that, in the parish where my home was, on a certain day in the year, the church-bell rang, and everybody went to receive a penny roll. Every child had one, and I recollect having mine. I claimed it as a privilege, because I was my father's son. I think there were six of us, who all had a roll; every child in the parish had one. So there are a number of privileges that come to us very early in our Christian life, and we mean to have them, first, because our Lord Jesus Christ has given us the right to have them; and, next, because, if we do not take what he bought for us, it will be robbing him, and wasting his substance. As he has paid for it all, and has given us the right to have it, let us take it.

You were put to school because you were a son. You did not like it; I daresay that you would rather have stopped at home at play. And you had a touch of the rod, sometimes, because you were a son. That was one of your privileges: "for what son is he whom the father chasteneth not?" One day you were in the street with other boys, doing wrong, and your father came along, and punished you. He did not touch your companions, for they were not his sons. You smile at those little things, and you did not at the time count your punishments as privileges; but they were. When the chastening of the Lord comes, call it a privilege, for that is what it is. There is no greater mercy that I know of on earth than good health except it be sickness; and that has often been a greater mercy to me than health.

It is a good thing to be without a trouble; but it is a better thing to have a trouble, and to know how to get grace enough to bear it. I am not so much afraid of the devil when he roars, as I am when he pretends to go to sleep. I think that, oftentimes, a roaring devil keeps us awake; and the troubles of this life stir us up to go to God in prayer, and that which looks to us ill turns to our good. "We know that all things work together for good to them that love God, to them who are the called according to his purpose."

III. Now I come to my last point, that is, A MATTER WHICH IS MYSTERIOUS. We are not only given the status of children, and the privilege of being called sons, but this mysterious matter is one of heavenly birth: "Which were born, not of blood, nor of the will of the flesh, nor of the will of man, but of God."

This new birth is *absolutely needful.* If we are ever to be numbered amongst God's children, we must be born again, born from above. We were born in sin, born children of wrath, even as others; to be God's children, it is absolutely necessary that we should be born again.

The change wrought thereby is *wonderfully radical.* It is not a mere outside washing, nor any touching up and repairing. It is a total renovation. Born again? I cannot express to you all that the change means, it is so deep, so thorough, so complete.

It is also *intensely mysterious.* What must it be to be born again? "I cannot understand it," says one. Nicodemus was a teacher in Israel, and he did not understand it. Does anybody understand it? Does anybody understand his first birth? What know we of it? And this second birth; some of us have passed through it, and know that we have, and remember well the pangs of that birth, yet we cannot describe the movements of the Spirit of God, by which we were formed anew, and made new creatures in Christ Jesus, according to that word from him who sits on the throne, "Behold, I make all things new!" It is a great mystery.

Certainly it is *entirely superhuman.* We cannot contribute to it. Man cannot make himself to be born again. His first birth is not of himself, and his second birth is not one jot more so. It is a work of the Holy Ghost, a work of God. It is a new creation; it is a quickening; it is a miracle from beginning to end.

Here is the point to which I call your special attention, it is *assuredly ours.* Many of us here have been born again. We know that we have, and herein lies the evidence of it, "As many as received him, to them gave he power to become the sons of God, even to them that believe on his name, which were born, not of blood, nor of the will of the flesh, nor of the will of man, but of God." If thou believest on Christ's name, thou art born of God. If thou hast received Christ into thy soul, thou hast obtained that birth that comes not of blood, nor of the will of parents, nor of the will of man, but of God. Thou hast passed from death unto life.

Let no man sit down here, and cover his face, and say, "There is no hope for me. I cannot understand about this new birth." If thou wilt take Christ, to have and to hold, henceforth and for ever, as thy sole trust and confidence, thou hast received that which no line of ancestors could ever give thee; for it is "not of blood." Thou dost possess that which no will of father and mother could ever give thee; for it is "not of the will of the flesh." Thou hast that which thine own will could not bring thee; for it is "not of the will of man." Thou hast that which only the Giver of life can bestow; for it is "of God." Thou art born again; for thou hast received Christ, and believed on his name. I do not urge you to look within, to try and see whether this new birth is there. Instead of looking within thyself, look thou to him who hangs on yonder cross, dying the Just for the unjust, to bring us to God. Fix thou thine eyes on him, and believe in him; and when thou seest in thyself much that is evil, look away to him; and when doubts prevail, look to him; and when thy conscience tells thee of thy past sins, look to him.

I have to go through this story almost every day of the year, and sometimes half a dozen times in a day. If there is a desponding soul anywhere within twenty miles, it will find me out, no matter whether I am at home, or at Mentone, or in any other part of the world. It will come from any distance, broken down, despairing, half insane sometimes; and I have no medicine to prescribe except "Christ, Christ, Christ; Jesus Christ and him crucified. Look away from yourselves, and trust in him." I go over and over and over with this, and never get one jot further, because I find that this medicine cures all soul sicknesses, while human quackery cures none. Christ alone is the one remedy for sin-sick souls. Receive him; believe on his name. We keep hammering at this. I can sympathize with Luther when he said, "I have preached justification by faith so often, and I feel sometimes that you are so slow to receive it, that I could almost take the Bible, and bang it about your heads." I am afraid that the truth would not have entered their hearts if he had done so. This is what we aim at, to get this one thought into a man, "Thou art lost, and therefore such an one as Christ came to save."

One said to me just lately, "Oh, sir, I am the biggest sinner that ever lived!" I replied, "Jesus Christ came into the world to save sinners." "But I have not any strength." "While we were yet without strength, in due time Christ died." "Oh! but," he said, "I have been utterly ungodly." "Christ died for the ungodly." "But I am lost." "Yes," I said, "This is a faithful saying, and worthy of all acceptation, that Christ Jesus came into the world to save sinners." "The Son of man has come to save that which was lost." I said to this man, "You have the brush in your hand, and at every stroke it looks as if you were quoting Scripture. You seem to be making yourself out to be the very man that Christ came to save. If you were to make yourself out to be good and excellent, I should give you this word—Jesus did not come to call the righteous, but sinners to repentance. He did not die for the good, but for the bad. He gave himself for our sins; he never gave himself for our righteousness. He is a Saviour. He has not come yet as a Rewarder of the righteous; that will be in his Second Advent. Now he comes as a great Forgiver of the guilty, and the only Saviour of the lost. Wilt thou come to him in that way?" "Oh! but," my friend said, "I have not anything to bring to Christ." "No," I said, "I know that you have not; but Christ has everything." "Sir," he said, "you do not know me, else you would not talk to me like this;" and I said, "No, and you do not know yourself, and you are worse than you think you are, though you think that you are bad enough in all conscience; but be you as bad as you may, Jesus Christ came on purpose to uplift from the dunghill those whom he sets among princes by his free, rich, sovereign grace."

Oh, come and believe in him, poor sinner! I feel that, if I had all your souls, I would believe in Christ for their salvation; I would trust him to save a million souls if I had them, for he is mighty to save. There can be no limit to his power to forgive. There can be no limit to the merit of his precious blood. There can be no boundary to the efficacy of his plea before the throne. Only trust him, and you must be saved. May his gracious Spirit lead you to do so now, for Christ's sake! Amen.